SHOCKED TO FAME

A COMEDY

COLIN A. MAYO

CONTENTS

CAST OF CHARACTERS
(IN ORDER OF APPEARANCE)

VARIOUS WOMEN: Non-speaking roles
THE CREEPER: ?
AMY DICK: Private Investigator.
RICK LITTLEWORTH: Employee at D. J. Butt, married to Lisa-Louise.
LISA-LOUISE LITTLEWORTH: Employee at Delavero's Estate Agents.
JARVIS DELAVERO: Son of Clive, employee at Delavero's.
ALEXA: Played by itself.
CLIVE DELAVERO: Owner/manager of Delavero's Estate agents.
P. C. MAXIMILIAN HEAD: Bedfordshire Police Officer.
RADIO PRESENTER A presenter to pre-record.
ANDREW CHARLES WITLOW: Employee at D. J. Butt, friend of Rick's.

The action takes place in front of the curtain; in Amy's office and in the Littleworth's front room/kitchenette.

TIME: THE PRESENT – November/December.

SETTING: The small town of Knobsworth, Bedfordshire.

GENRE: Jet black comedy.

*This play contains very strong language as well as numerous sexual references – therefore it is only suitable for an **ADULT** audience.*

Shot to fame,
Shot to fame,
It's in the name,
It's in the name,
Sadness reigns
When you're shocked to fame. (Anon)

Duran Duran's version of David Bowie's "Fame" plays as the
audience takes their seats.

ACT 1

SCENE ONE

ACT 1

Scene One

The curtain is closed, a woman walks across the stage. A figure bursts out between the curtains, he is wearing a gimp suit which covers his body and face. He scares the woman who runs off. Exit stage left. *David Bowie's song "Fashion" starts playing. The figure calmly walks to the edge of the stage and performs a dance to the music whilst standing on the spot, moving from side to side. Then he too runs off.* Exit stage right.

The music fades.

The curtain opens

Thursday – midday.

AMY DICK'S *office. This contains a desk with a chair behind it and a chair in front of it (DR). There is a door (RC) near to the desk. At this point the stage is partitioned by another curtain/lighting closing off a portion of the back of the stage. There is a leather sofa to the side of the desk (C), there is also a television with its back to the audi-*

*ence by the desk – opposite the sofa. In the corner (LC), there is a low cabinet by another door (UL). Littered around the room are little numbered golf flags which indicate **AMY** has made her office into a putting green. There is a golf trolley and clubs near the door (UL). On the desk is a sign that reads: "Amy Dick – Private Investigator". When the curtain draws back, she is practicing putting on the carpet, in front of the sofa, and standing with a putter in a golf stance, facing the audience, a golf ball is at her feet.*

AMY *(singing Fashion):* We are the goon squad and we're coming to town, Beep-beep.

(to self but out loud) They don't write lyrics like that anymore.

there is a knock on the door.

Come in.

there is a knock on the door.

(louder): Come in!

RICK LITTLEWORTH *walks in. He is nervous. He is wearing a black, leather biker jacket and carrying a motorcycle helmet. He has a day sack over his shoulder.*

AMY *does not even turn around; she is concentrating on her putt.*

AMY: Just put it down on the cabinet by the door.

RICK LITTLEWORTH *(he coughs and moves awkwardly from foot to foot – unsure of whether or not to walk further into the room).*

Sorry…

AMY: *AMY turns and looks at **RICK**.*

Apologies, I thought you were an Amazon delivery – I'm expecting some golf club covers.

RICK: Have I come to the right place? It's hard to find being above a shop and up all those stairs.

AMY: Well, that depends what you're looking for, if it's fruit and veg you're after then you'd be better off at the Aldi around the corner.

RICK: I mean, you're a private eye, aren't you?

AMY folds her club under her arm.

AMY: Indeed, I am, Amy Dick's the name. I come from a long line of Dicks.

RICK: Oh good. I saw your advert on the internet and I thought you may be able to…. I mean… I've not done this sort of thing before… but I'm hoping you can help. I'm Rick… Rick Littleworth.

RICK offers his hand but AMY doesn't take it.

AMY: Well, take a seat, Rick, and I'll see what I can do for you.

RICK takes off his leather motorcycle jacket and sits on the sofa. He places his crash helmet and the day sack on the floor.

I meant on the chair…. Oh, never mind…

AMY is frustrated by the fact that she has not finished her putt – she feels RICK is going to waste her time.

RICK: I've taken a day off work… I've been meaning to come to see you for ages… and I've finally plucked up the courage…. I think my wife's having an affair.

AMY: I see, and you want me to gather the evidence to help you file for divorce…

AMY walks around to her side of the desk, she places the putter by her chair, leaning it on the edge of her desk.

RICK: I just want to know... it's the not knowing that's the worst thing... it is eating me up inside.

AMY: OK. Have you seen my charges? I charge £55 per hour and I need a retainer, after that there are expenses and additional costs depending on how involved the work is.

(*mimicking Groucho Marx*) *Those are my prices and if you don't like them... well, I have others.*

RICK: Pardon me?

AMY: Sorry, I'm a film buff, that's what Groucho Marx said about "principles". "Those are my principles" …. Oh dear… never mind… anyway, my prices are fixed.

RICK: Yes, yes, I saw your website, I'm happy to pay anything... I've come into quite a bit of money... (*he stops abruptly*). I just need to know...

AMY gets an A4 notepad from the desk drawer and picks up a pen.

AMY: We just have to go through some preliminaries and then we'll get started. Name?

RICK: Rick... Rick Littleworth.

AMY: Address?

RICK: 14, Riverside, Knobsworth.

AMY: Oh, those houses by the woods and the golf course?

RICK: Yes, I'm not sure where the river is though.

AMY: You probably won't find out until it floods. When were you born?

RICK: On my birthday.

AMY: I meant the date.

RICK: Oh sorry, 6th June, 1975.

AMY: Thirty-one years after D-Day. That makes you forty-four. Nationality?

RICK: Is that relevant?

AMY: No, but everyone seems to ask it these days.

RICK: Manx.

AMY: Pardon me?

RICK: I was born on the Isle of Man whilst my parents were on holiday there. Father was mad keen on motorcycling and we went there every year to watch the Isle of Man TT – one-time Mother gave birth to me – I was premature - but I was raised in Bedfordshire...

AMY: Let's put you down as British, shall we? Married, how long?

RICK: Fourteen years.

AMY: That's good, you've beaten the seven-year itch by a factor of two. Children?

RICK: No.

AMY: Choice, impotence or incompetence?

RICK: Well... er... er...

AMY: It's OK you don't have to answer that, it's sometimes a factor that's all...

RICK: In what?

AMY: Infidelity.

RICK: I see. Will it take long?

AMY: Oh no, just a few more questions and then I'll take some details of your suspicions.

RICK: No, I mean to find out.

AMY: It shouldn't take more than a week or so; these days, with social media, nothing's secret for long. Everyone leaves a carbon footprint.

RICK: Don't you mean a data footprint?

AMY: That too, but I drive an electric car. What about you?

RICK: I have a Honda motorbike – a CB 300R – which I use for work and a 1975 Norton Commando 850cc Roadster (*he tries to make a joke*) – it's as old as me but in a lot better condition.

AMY: That's good – more of a thumb print than a footprint – everyone should think of the environment. I take it your wife partakes?

RICK: In what?

AMY(*frustrated*): In social media, what do you think I meant?

RICK: Oh yes. She's on Facebook, Snapchat, Twitter, WhatsApp, Instagram...

AMY: What about you?

RICK: I've no friends. No one would be interested in my tweets. People say I'm boring... useless...

AMY(*ignoring his self-pity*): I don't do social media myself but then I see the dark side of it – anyway, unlike the rest of the populous, I like to keep my pubic life private.

RICK: I see... I bet you get a lot of people like me?

AMY: If you mean divorces and infidelity – well yes – matrimonials are my peaches and cream. Plus, a bit of internal company fraud where the company doesn't want police involvement due to reputational damage. Missing persons, that's always a good one and I.T's on the increase: investigating fraud on-line; email and phone forensics; also trolling that sort of thing but unfortunately, I'm not great with computers. Hark, that's why you don't see one here! I prefer a pen and paper... or a quill and parchment if there's any to hand... but my brother helps me out where that's concerned so I'm not completely I.T deficient.

RICK: But you think you can help me, do you?

AMY: I know so, if you want proof, or otherwise, of your wife's affair then I'm your man – only I'm a woman – women are a lot better at this game then men – a lot better. They're more subtle; they can get people to open up; they can disguise themselves easier; they're more sensitive to their surroundings - so you'll be pleased you selected a female Private Investigator over a male one – rest assured of that. A lot of women work in this area now – probably more women than men – women are better at the whole secrecy thing. The days of Humphrey Bogart, with a cigarette hanging out of his mouth, wearing a trilby and a dirty Mac, are long gone.

RICK: Great. I'm not sexist. I knew from your name you were a woman – well Amy – that's a woman's name, right? And that didn't put me off, not at all.

AMY: Good shout, Rick, good shout. Now, what do you do for a living?

RICK: I'm an accountant... well, I say accountant... (*laughs nervously*) that's a bit posh ... I'm a clerk who does the books in small engineering company – I'm a bookkeeper really – I did A.A.T qualifications - Levels 1, 2 and 3.

AMY: A. A. T stands for?

RICK: Association of Accounting Technicians.

AMY: That's good, so you have qualifications. Qualifications help in life – although they can be a hinder-ance if you have the wrong ones.

RICK *places his head in his hands, talks to the floor.*

RICK: It's the not knowing that's the worst thing – the suspicion; the deceit, the lack of trust… it's tearing me apart. Lisa-Louise was my life, now I feel she's slipping through my fingers… I don't want to confront her… that would be too much… I just want to know… I'm making plans, I've got a plan.

AMY: Tell me a bit about your wife then: age, job that sort of thing.

RICK: Well, she's forty-six – the same age as me – she works for a family run estate agent firm – Delavero's – you've probably heard of them, they're big in Knobsworth. She earns more than me – a lot more – plus commission – she's good at sales - she often works late and weekends.

AMY: A normal lot for an estate agent. What's her date of birth?

RICK: 12th October, 1975.

AMY: OK – and what makes you think she's playing away?

RICK: She's out a lot – she doesn't tell me where she's going. She's got high-priced jewellery…new clothes, new lingerie… recently she had an expensive set of earrings and a necklace for her birthday – she said the Delavero's staff had had a collection and bought them for her – but I'm not so sure.

AMY: And how long has this been going on?

RICK: I don't know – at least six months I should think – probably longer.

AMY: Anything else?

RICK: She takes calls on her mobile and speaks quietly – I hear her say things like – *I can't speak now.*

AMY: Any other suspicions?

RICK: Her manager, Clive, who owns Delavero's - well she's always liked him – he's divorced – she talks a lot about him – well, I say that, she used to but now she clams up.

AMY: OK, do you have a recent photograph of your wife?

RICK *picks up his day sack – he takes out a magazine – Classic Bike, he flicks through the pages and takes a large photograph from inside and passes it to **AMY**.*

AMY *looks at it and then at **RICK**, she looks back at the photograph and then back at **RICK** and then she hands the photograph back.*

Where did you meet her?

RICK: At a car boot sale in Rickmansworth – I was buying – she was selling – her first husband, Darren, had recently died in a jet-ski accident whilst they were holidaying in Fuerteventura - she was selling off some of his old clothes and other bits and pieces as she wanted to move on - too many ghosts I suppose. Well, the suits were good quality and a perfect fit. She had only bought down a small sample, but she gave me her phone number and asked me to call her. I did. I cleared out the whole of Darren's wardrobe – (*he tugs at the sleeve of his shirt*) in fact, this is one of his Ben Sherman's.

AMY(*looking surprised*): And you asked her out on a date?

RICK: Well, to be honest, I didn't, I thought she was well out of my league – she made the first move. I was on my own too – never been married – had my own place which I'd inherited from my mother – she had dementia. I cared for her till she died. Only child, you see.

AMY: So you started courting?

RICK: Yes, Lisa-Louise wanted us to start again with a new property so we bought another house together and then 14 Riverside – I wanted somewhere quiet and, as we've got no children, a bungalow suited us just fine.

AMY: And you suspect she's having an affair with Clive Delavero?

RICK: No, not necessarily.

AMY (*frustrated*): Well, who then?

RICK: It could be his son, Jarvis, he's twenty-six and he works in the same office – he stands to inherit. I know he's always liked her – she's joked about it – how she attracts the younger men…

AMY: My word.

RICK: Also, there's this accountant who pays visits to their office – I don't know his real name – only his nickname – Spud – I know one night he and Lisa-Louise were at Delavero's alone – she didn't get in until the early hours…

AMY: So we have Clive Delavero, his son, Jarvis Delavero and the accountant, Spud, as possible lovers…

(*Pause*)

RICK: There's also an electrician who comes

around – Reg "Sparky" Hughes – he's always liked Lisa-Louise. We had to have our house re-wired you see. The time he took – well, he could have done the whole of Knobsworth.

AMY: Blimey, it's a good job the Tories reduced the British Army down to six service personnel, an armoured carrier and a kit bag as we might be looking for a needle in a wool pack.

RICK: It's not her fault – it's me. I've never been good at anything. Everything I do turns to rust – life's just been one long kick in the balls. I don't blame her for having an affair. I'm useless.

AMY(*surprised*): Goodness.

RICK gets up and walks DC as he does so he steps over AMY'S miniature golf flags.

RICK: My Dad had low expectations of me – he thought I was hopeless and expected nothing from me – unfortunately I didn't disappoint him.

AMY: I see, and this is getting us where exactly?

RICK: I think you need to know a bit about me, Ms Dick – know why I don't blame Lisa-Louise for wanting someone else – I've always known she could do a lot better than me. A lot better. I've always thought she'd leave me. To be honest, I'm surprised she's stayed as long as she has. I'm just no good.

AMY: Good Lord, you really do have some self-esteem issues, don't you?

RICK(*annoyed, angry*): What do you expect! Dad belittled me, put me down, said I would amount to nothing. I know he wanted a daughter because he was one of seven brothers.

AMY: My, that sounds like the plot of a musical.

RICK: Don't try to be funny, Ms Dick, I'm not in the mood for people being funny – I think you'll find I'm an extremely serious person. I'm telling you my life story and I expect respect.

AMY: Goodness. OK. It's very interesting.

RICK: As I was saying Dad was the runt of the litter – as you can imagine some of his brothers were almost old enough to be his father – well, he was put down and bullied by them and then, when he became a parent, he took it out on me.

AMY: It's usually the way. Adulthood is often just a postscript to childhood.

RICK: You're so right, Ms Dick.

AMY: Sorry to interrupt but didn't your Dad want a boy – rather than a girl - to carry forward the Little-worth family name, I mean?

RICK: Ms Dick, that's so last century – now there's all sorts of partnerships and permutations between the sexes.

AMY: But not when you were born.

RICK: I know and maybe it wouldn't have mattered if I hadn't been an only child but Father became sterile a year after my birth. By all accounts he contracted syphilis from a careless prostitute in Amsterdam.

AMY: Blimey, you do like to open up! Talk about washing your family's dirty saucepans in public!

RICK: I've got no one to talk to – no one under-stands me - you seem to be the listening type. There's something about you, Ms Dick – something that makes people want to talk - but it's only you listening to me, isn't it?

AMY: Of course! Who the Hell else would want to listen to this…this…this… tragic and compelling family saga?

RICK looks around. He goes to AMY's desk, leans on it. He looks at her. He looks out to the audience. He looks back at AMY.

RICK(*whispers*): Good, you've not got the place bugged then? You being a private eye an' all.

AMY: The place isn't bugged but if I wanted to record you, without you knowing, I could do it very, very easily but I don't.

RICK: Why? Why ever not? Aren't I interesting enough for you?

AMY: No, it's not that relevant to the case you've asked me to investigate.

RICK: Oh, so I *am* boring! I bet I'm the only person in Britain who owns a smart TV which *doesn't* send data back to China.

AMY: Look, Rick, if you want to get it off your lungs be my guest. I charge by the hour - £55 as I say. But I have to warn you I close in four hours' time…

RICK starts pacing the office – DC and DL.

RICK: Thank you, Ms Dick.

I went to a bog standard comprehensive - the type everyone goes to unless they're clever, rich or lucky. I left with minimal Q's. My parents were a lot older than the other parents – and my Mother was ten years older than my Father. At school I was picked on and bullied. People used to say "is your grandmother collecting you from school today?" when in fact it was my Mother.

I remember going up to my best mate, Aaron Avery, and asking him if I could join in a game, do you know what he said?

AMY shakes her head – words have failed her.

"Fuck off, Littleworth."

AMY: How old were you?

RICK: Seven, eight... maybe nine...

AMY: And you still harbour a grudge because this chap Avery gave you the bird?

RICK: But it wasn't just that – all my life I've been a loser, I've been sacked from jobs; I've had disciplinary action taken against me and women have rejected me. I've been in nightclubs and bars and I've tried to chat up women but all I've ever got was the cold shoulder: I've had more blow outs than the Michelin Man rolling over a bed of nails.

AMY: Gosh.

RICK: After I left school, I did a number of boring jobs – mainly office based. I lived at home. When I was twenty my Father died – that syphilis certainly has a nasty sting in its tail. I was a nobody in a sea of nobodies.

AMY: So basically, you were like everyone else?

RICK: It was just me and my Mother after that but her dementia came on quickly after my Father's death. I looked after her for eight years until she died – Lisa-Louise always says I've no conversation but when you've been with someone all day who says:

Have we had dinner?

Did we go shopping?

The populations getting older and toilets are getting less.

How old ~~and~~ am I?

How old are you?

Are you married?

Do you live here?

Have you been to work today?

What day is it?

What month are we in?

And ends with…the worst thing any parent can say to their off-spring…

Who the Hell are you?

It's a blooming nightmare. It's constant and so, so repetitive. It was a bit like living with Jeremy Paxman on speed. Around and around, she went like a washing machine.

RICK *stands at the front of the stage, facing the audience and moves his head around as he talks.*

Around and around like a washing machine.

Repeating and repeating and repeating.

(*pause*)

Around and around like a washing machine.

Repeating and repeating and repeating.

(*pause*)

Around and around like a washing machine.

Repeating and repeating and repeating.

until I could take no more.

AMY: So what did you do?

RICK: I did the A.A.T Levels 1, 2 and 3 in bookkeeping. It was a distance learning course - I studied whilst I listened to mother.

AMY: Well, that's good… an interest.

RICK: Then Mother died, I inherited the house and then I met Lisa-Louise, she was my dream, my life - I worshipped her. She was out of my league – I knew that (*tearful*) – I couldn't believe it when she accepted my proposal of marriage but even that went wrong… (*pause*) – why does life give you so much flipping opportunity to fantasise about what might have been?

RICK *sits back down on the sofa. He takes a handkerchief from his trouser pocket and dabs his eyes.*

AMY: Where… where… where were you?

RICK: When?

AMY: When you proposed?

RICK: On Camber Sands, down on one knee with the tide rolling in… my trousers were wet right through, and I got house maid's knee but I didn't care – I was happy.

AMY: Romantic.

I'm no expert but it sounds to me like you have an inferiority complex, Rick.

RICK: Yes, yes, I have.

Now *AMY* *gets up, she picks up her putter and walks around her desk, she is holding the putter under her arm like a Sergeant Major grasping a baton, she walks up and down for the rest of the scene – neatly stepping over her golf flags.* *RICK* *is now prostrate on the sofa.*

AMY: Have you tried self-help books? *Every day, in every way I'm getting better and better* – that sort of thing.

RICK: Yes, they don't work.

AMY: To be honest, I always thought that stuff was a load of bollocks. If they worked everyone would be successful.

RICK: I try to put their words into action, they fail and I feel even worse than I did at the start.

AMY: You're bound too. The authors are just preying on people's insecurities. Perhaps, rather than paying me to investigate your wife's possible infidelity, you need to seek out a counsellor?

RICK: I've had more counsellors' than a skip load of A Listers and I'm still messed up.

AMY: What about religion, that can help?

RICK: Mother was a Catholic. Devout. I used to go to church with her on a Wednesday and a Sunday. Then she forgot who Jesus and the Virgin Mary were – she thought they were an item and that annoyed Father Mulholland. He'd obviously missed the excellent dementia awareness course run by the Roman Catholic church... I'm lapsed now because of it.

AMY: That's the trouble with religion – very unforgiving.

RICK: I did briefly join a small, but not insignificant charity, called C.A.D.

AMY: Computer Aided Design?

RICK: No, Catholics Against Dementia. I used to collect on their behalf but I became disillusioned.

AMY: Why?

RICK: People only give to charities to feel good about themselves - not to help others.

AMY: Profound and possibly true but surely, they're doing both, aren't they?

RICK: I suppose so. But I didn't see it like that and the people who ran the charity seemed to pay themselves a lot of money out of the donations us volunteers collected.

AMY: Rule Number One for the people at the top is to make sure that the people at the top have a comfortable life. It's always the way. Sorry, you were saying?

RICK *is still laying on the sofa.*

RICK: Well, Mother died and left everything to me. Except this Dutch charity that supported prostitutes – fallen women as Mother used to call them – she felt guilty on Father's behalf: being a Catholic opens up an artic lorry load of opportunities to feel guilty about everything and anything but doing it on some else's behalf is about as good as it gets.

AMY: Yes, very true, Rick.

RICK: They were called Working Women of Amsterdam Need Knowledge and Skills.

AMY: Isn't the acronym W.W.A.N.K.S?

RICK: Yes, W.W.A.N.K.S. it sounds better in Dutch. Anyway, she made them a handy donation.

AMY: God, this is a tale of woe. Are you sure you want a private investigator?

RICK: Yes, Ms Dick, Yes, Yes. Why do you ask?

AMY: Well, I think you need help in other areas - have you tried Delia Smith?

RICK: She's a sodding chef for Heaven's Sake!

AMY: Yes, but you are what you eat, so they say, maybe if you changed your diet you would change your outlook on life. Just a thought. A souffle would be a snowflake and a raw steak a red-blooded, confident male – that sort of thing.

RICK(*frustrated – sudden burst of anger – sits up*): Look Ms Dick, it wouldn't work for God's Sake. Now, are you going to help me or not? If you want, I'll take my business elsewhere!

AMY: Yes, yes, of course I'll help, just pay me the retainer which is £100 and I'll bill you for expenses and time - you can pay the rest when my work is done. The only thing I need from you is your front door key.

RICK: Why?

AMY: Because, Mr Littleworth, I may have to conduct some field work in your house. I don't like doing it, but I like to have all my hens in a row before I start shafting them.

RICK: Alright then.

RICK stands up, he goes to his trouser pocket and takes a key off a key ring. He hands it to **AMY** who has returned to her desk.

I've a spare one in the garage. Lisa-Louise won't suspect a thing.

AMY: Good. I think I have all the essentials, but I do recommend that you to do some work on your self-esteem.

RICK: What sort of work?

AMY: Inflation. It sounds to me that you've more hang-up's than a cave full of bats. I think you need to address it, Mr Littleworth, as a matter of urgency. Low self-esteem is a very, very serious problem which will continue to affect your future happiness.

RICK: OK, thank you Ms Dick and I'm sorry I lost

my temper earlier – it's all too much, you see, the strain. I feel really tense right now. I know Lisa-Louise and I haven't been getting on but the thought of her with another man... well... it's sending me around the twist.

AMY: I hope I can assist.

RICK: I really appreciate the fact you have heard me out and tried to give me advice.

AMY: Thanks for the compliments but the only ones that count come in cash.

RICK puts his motorcycle jacket back on and takes a bulging wallet from his inside pocket. He counts some notes out and places them on AMY'S desk. She passes him a receipt. He picks up his day sack and his crash helmet and he makes his way to the door (UL).

RICK: Thank you again, Ms Dick. I do so hope you can help me.

Curtain

ACT 1
SCENE 2

SATURDAY EVENING

The Littleworth's front room/kitchenette. When the front and rear curtains are pulled back it reveals a living room scene. Behind the second curtain is a kitchenette with a breakfast bar (UR/UC) – on top of which rests an Alexa; there is also another door (UR) which has a white "black-out" blind over the window – this leads to the Littleworth's garage and the blind is on the garage side. The desk has been replaced by a table and more chairs added and the leather sofa has been moved around so it faces the audience – also a coffee table has been placed in front of the sofa, along with a rug. The golfing paraphernalia has been removed.

LISA-LOUISE(*off-stage*): I'm pleased they all finally went home and just left us in the Red Lion – they serve tasty food their too – saves cooking. It's just a pity we can't go back to your Dad's house – I never like... well... you know...

JARVIS(*off stage*): My step-sister and her boyfriend are home tonight – she's cooking him dinner - and

24

Dad could be in at any time. He doesn't know about us (*he laughs*) - I can't wait to tell him.

LISA-LOUISE(*off stage*): Best not do that.

JARVIS(*off stage*): Why not?

LISA-LOUISE(*off stage*): I don't think he'd approve, and he *is* my manager, remember?

JARVIS(*off stage*): Shall I take my shoes off.

LISA-LOUISE(*off stage*): No, you're alright. I'm not taking mine off.

LISA-LOUISE enters the living room (UL) followed by JARVIS. LISA-LOUISE puts her handbag and coat down by the interior door. JARVIS is wearing an expensive suit; he fidgets and looks nervous. LISA-LOUISE is wearing a dark business skirt/suit and high-heeled shoes. JARVIS smiles inanely.

LISA-LOUISE:Do you want a drink, Jarvis?

JARVIS: Just a fresh Coke, please – straight out of the can – no ice or lemon.

LISA-LOUISE goes to the back of the stage (UR/UC) and around the breakfast bar and into the kitchenette.

LISA-LOUISE: Alexa, play soft, romantic pop music from the 1990's.

ALEXA: *Playing soft, romantic 1990's pop music from the Amazon music playlist.*

Alexa starts to play Madness' It Must Be Love – a re-issued hit from 1992. LISA-LOUISE collects a Coke from the fridge and makes herself a Gin and Tonic. As she does this JARVIS is facing the audience jogging from foot to foot. He decides to take off his suit jacket and carefully puts it over the back of a chair. Then he loosens his tie and undoes a few buttons and then he does them back up. He *does a bit of shadow boxing. Suddenly a head bobs up at the kitchen window and looks in. It is **AMY**. She sees **LISA-LOUISE** in the kitchen and drops back down. **LISA-LOUISE** returns to the living room with a can of Coke, she is also carrying her Gin and Tonic, she hands the can of Coke to **JARVIS**.*

LISA-LOUISE: Cheers.

*The glass and can touch. **AMY's** head appears at the window again and then disappears.*

JARVIS: It's a nice place you've got here. It's big for a bungalow.

LISA-LOUISE: Yes, when I met Rick... well, let's just say I had a windfall from my dead husband's life insurances plus we had a house to sell whilst Rick inherited his mother's place – he was an only child. It meant we could pool resources and buy quite a nice property. This is our second house together without a mortgage – the first one was on a busy main road – Rick wanted somewhere quieter, more secluded. He doesn't like people watching him. He's paranoid like that.

JARVIS: How many bedrooms?

LISA-LOUISE: Two.

JARVIS: Toilets?

LISA-LOUISE: Two, one en suite. Do you want a tour?

JARVIS: No, not yet. I like to picture a dwelling in my mind's eye before I see it in the flesh. I saw you had an integral garage. It's a strange design – I'm guessing the back wall of the garage is there and that's the door to it.

(*JARVIS* points to the second door (UR) which is now revealed, it is in the kitchen area.)

LISA-LOUISE: Yes that's right! You certainly know your stuff! Rick uses it as a workshop. The previous owners built the bungalow but there wasn't much space for it to be positioned facing the road so the garage and drive point towards the road and the front door is around the side as you know – then, if you go through that door...

(*LISA-LOUISE* points to the second door (RC))

you enter the hallway which leads onto the bathroom which is next to the garage and the two bedrooms – our one – the bigger one - is at the back – or the side depending how you look at it.

JARVIS: It's an unusual but functional design making the best of a limited plot size - I can see that – when you say that Rick uses the garage as a workshop, what does he work on?

LISA-LOUISE: Oh, engines and this and that. He has a work bench and an old, double - doored wardrobe in there which my late husband and I had in our bedroom. Sometimes he stores both his bikes in the garage.

JARVIS: His bikes? Is he a Lycra lout?

LISA-LOUISE(*laughs*): No, his motorbikes. He has a Norton Commando classic motorbike which is his pride and joy and a Honda which he uses for work.

JARVIS: I see, a bit of a man cave, then?

LISA-LOUISE: Yes, I just leave him to it. He sits in there for hours listening to the radio and working on engines or polishing his Norton.

JARVIS: What does he listen to?

LISA-LOUISE: Oh, I don't know - Classic FM, LBC, that sort of thing. Why?

JARVIS: I'm trying to get a picture of your husband in my mind's eye. Not just a picture but a warts and all portrait. Really get a feel for the man.

LISA-LOUISE: Is that necessary?

JARVIS: Well, if I'm going to be committing adultery with his wife, I'd like to know the strength of the opposition.

LISA-LOUISE: No worries there – Rick's deflated.

JARVIS: Good. Not that he'd be any match for me. I'm in the peak of physical condition.

(*JARVIS waits for LISA-LOUISE to concur with this view – whilst he waits he places the can down on the coffee table and once more indulges in a bit of shadow boxing - when she doesn't say anything, he says the first thing that comes into his head.*)

What football team does he support?

LISA-LOUISE: He doesn't like football.

JARVIS: Odd.

LISA-LOUISE: "Odd" is Rick's middle name.

JARVIS(*without irony*): I thought it was Malcolm.

(*beat*)

But let me get this straight, so I'm clear in my own mind, neither of you use the garage for what it was intended for?

LISA-LOUISE: No, I always park the company car on the drive, if I bring it home, but, as you know, I mostly leave it at work.

JARVIS: If I had a garage, I'd park a car in it.

LISA-LOUISE: I don't mind leaving my car outside, as you say its Rick's man cave.

JARVIS: Yes, but a garage should be used for storing cars.

LISA-LOUISE: All cars have glove compartments, how many people put gloves in them?

JARVIS: Point taken Lisa; you have an answer for everything.

LISA-LOUISE: I have to working for Delavero's.

JARVIS: You say you have two good sized bedrooms?

LISA-LOUISE: Yes, one's for guests.

JARVIS: Nice. Good area of Knobsworth too – by the golf course – backing onto woods - must be looking at £550,000 - minimum. Bungalows are always very popular, especially with an aging population. It's the lack of stairs see. The old folks can't get up 'um and if they do, they can't get back down 'um.

LISA-LOUISE(*laughs*): Jarvis, do you ever switch off that little estate agent button in your head?

JARVIS: No, it's in the blood, Dad was always analysing property, I've inherited the gene.

LISA-LOUISE: And also the randy gene.

JARVIS(*smiles smugly*): Yeh, though somehow, I don't think I'll ever be quite like him.

LISA-LOUISE: Meaning?

JARVIS: A womaniser.

LISA-LOUISE: I would hope not, Jarvis. That's *not* a good trait.

JARVIS: You succumbed to his wicked ways.

LISA-LOUISE: After a while... he *is* charming...

and very confident… he has that way about him. He's a gentleman.

JARVIS: All the women say that. He bedded one of my girlfriend's once – she was thirty years his junior.

LISA-LOUISE: That's not nice, do you know how many girlfriends he's had?

JARVIS: Too many.

LISA-LOUISE: I just hope he…

JARVIS: What?

LISA-LOUISE: Nothing…well, it's not nice to be cheated on. Come on, Jarvis, sit down.

*They move to the leather sofa and sit down. **AMY's** head appears at the window again – she takes in the scene – all she can see is the back of their heads. She stands up so the audience can see her and then moves towards the front door (UL).*

LISA-LOUISE: What was that?

JARVIS *now has his arms around **LISA-LOUISE**. She has kicked off her shoes.*

JARVIS: Probably someone delivering leaflets for pizzas we get them all the time around our place.

LISA-LOUISE: It sounded like the door…

JARVIS(*hollow laugh*): It's not Rick, is it?

LISA-LOUISE: No, I never see him these days, he's always out… particularly on Saturday nights.

JARVIS(*raises his arms and wriggles his hands like a ghost*): whoa, whoa, you don't think he's The Creeper, do you?

LISA-LOUISE *playfully hits him with a cushion.*

LISA-LOUISE: No! Don't be daft. Rick's a nice guy but he's as about as effective as a fist with no thumb.

JARVIS: Why did you marry him then?

LISA-LOUISE: I felt sorry for him... and he was very sympathetic... he caught me at a low ebb, what with Darren dying in a jet ski accident and everything, it was such a shock – I mean, you don't expect to go on holiday and lose your other half, do you? I felt lonely, vulnerable...

JARVIS: Yeh, I can see that... did... did... did the travel insurance pay out?

LISA-LOUISE: Yes, and the life insurance too – that was the one saving grace – doubling up on the insurances like that – I always take out comprehensive travel insurance too – I never go anywhere unless I'm fully protected. Mind you I was a bit disappointed with Ryan Air when I flew back to Luton.

JARVIS: Why?

LISA-LOUISE: Well, when I returned home the seat next to me – Darren's seat – had been sold to another passenger which I thought was a bit off.

JARVIS: In the airline industry wasted space is wasted money.

LISA-LOUISE: I suppose so; you're right as usual, Jarvis.

JARVIS: You meet Rick soon after?

LISA-LOUISE: Yes, Rick's mother had just died as well... it kind of bonded us.

JARVIS: You've got me now.

LISA-LOUISE: Yes, I've got you.

JARVIS: I'll look after you.

LISA-LOUISE: Says the twenty-six-year-old who lives at home with his Dad.

JARVIS: You know what I mean. I'll protect you from The Creeper, look after you like that. Make sure no one gets near you who can do you harm...

JARVIS and LISA-LOUISE start kissing, a digital SLR camera appears over the small cabinet near to the door (LC). AMY has entered the house and is taking photographs from behind the cabinet. There's a flash – AMY falls back on the floor whispering.

AMY(*under her breath*): Shit, shit, shit – I forgot to turn the flash off.

LISA-LOUISE(*panicking*): What was that? Jarvis! What was that?

JARVIS: A flash of lightening that was all - don't worry Lisa... (*he pats her hand condescendingly*) ... don't worry.

LISA-LOUISE: They didn't say there was going to be rain.

JARVIS: Ah, but you can have lightening without rain. Our weather is all up in the air these days – the meteorologists never get it right (*laughs*). Blimey, if they say it'll rain, I wear shorts and a vest; if they say it will be sunny, I take my umbrella and if they say it'll snow, I slap on sun cream.

They both laugh.

Take it from me, Lisa, experts know fuck-all.

LISA-LOUISE: I'm beginning to think no one knows anything anymore - so perhaps you're right. I thought it came from over there, that's all (*she points towards the small cabinet behind which AMY lurks*).

JARVIS: Diffraction – as soon as I saw this place I thought – "*now this is a bungalow that suffers diffraction of the light"* – you have so many big windows, you see, and being South facing – well, it stands to reason. The flash of lightening hits the glass at the wrong angle, it does a pirouette, takes a few hair bends and lands anywhere in the room. It's science, see?

LISA-LOUISE: You certainly know your stuff, Jarvis, but we're overshadowed by trees – we live near woods.

JARVIS: Light moves in mysterious ways, Lisa.

LISA-LOUISE: Does it, indeed, you're so very clever, clever, clever – I could just eat you right up.

LISA-LOUISE *starts snuggling up to* ***JARVIS*** *but he moves away – he would rather hold court.*

JARVIS: I'm not a one trick pony if that's what you mean. Dad made sure I had a very broad education – I could have gone to Uni but I wanted to get stuck into the estate agent business. I thought to myself *'Jarvis – the sooner you get stuck in to it, then sooner you'll make your mark on the business and make an enviable amount of money."* I guess people would call me ambitious.

LISA-LOUISE: I guess they would.

JARVIS: But I wasn't born with a silver spoon – oh no - Dad made sure I've had to work every step of the way – no special privileges, no extra bonuses, just me and my estate agent prowess.

LISA-LOUISE: You've done well for yourself.

LISA-LOUISE *again leans into him, snuggles on the sofa.*

Umm, it's nice listening to you, Jarvis; Rick can't hold a knife and fork yet alone a conversation.

JARVIS: A lot of people have said I'm a good

conversationalist, especially for one so young. I'm like a sponge, see. I just absorb information. I know a lot about a lot of things. A lot of people have been surprised by how much I know. You ask me something – anything at all – and I'll tell you something about it.

LISA-LOUISE: Not now Jarvis, I just want to hold you.

JARVIS takes off his tie and starts to undo his shirt. He throws the tie on the floor.

JARVIS: It's hot in here, isn't it?

LISA-LOUISE: I guess it's the windows. The def... whatever you called it.

JARVIS: Diffraction - See, you're learning from me.

JARVIS and LISA-LOUISE start to embrace. Clothes start to come off. A digital SLR camera appears over the top of the cabinet (LC) and AMY takes photographs.

LISA-LOUISE: I love the younger man – you're so fit and muscular.

JARVIS: I work out, keep in shape. A lot of people have been impressed by my body.

LISA-LOUISE(*embracing JARVIS*): I know I certainly am.

JARVIS: Has Dad got a nice body?

LISA-LOUISE: It's a bit flabby and going to seed, not toned like yours.

JARVIS: And Spud?

LISA-LOUISE(*annoyed*): How the Hell should I know?

JARVIS: Oh, sorry... I just thought...

LISA-LOUISE: It was once, alright? I'd had a drink

… he'd bought a bottle of wine… it was a mistake…and yes, his body needs toning up too.

JARVIS: Has Rick got a nice body?

LISA-LOUISE: No. He's the original Mr Puniverse.

JARVIS: But he's a nice guy, right?

LISA-LOUISE: Yes, he's a nice guy…

JARVIS(*laughs*): Dad always says nice guys come second.

LISA-LOUISE(*under her breath*): If they come at all.

JARVIS: Do you love me just for my body then?

LISA-LOUISE: I like you Jarvis and I like your body. Let's just leave it like that for the moment. I don't want any pressure, OK?

*They renew their embrace – **AMY** continues her photography. At last they break off. **AMY** ducks behind the cabinet.*

JARVIS: Like but not love…?

LISA-LOUISE: It's too early…. Come on, I think it's time we danced! Follow me. I love this one.

Alexa, turn the volume up.

***LISA-LOUISE** takes **JARVIS** by the hand and tugs him off the sofa.*

It's one of my favourites. It reminds of…of… being young…

*Alexa starts to play Robson & Jerome's Unchained Melody - a hit from 1995 when **LISA-LOUISE** was twenty. **LISA-LOUISE** puts her arms around an uncomfortable looking **JARVIS**.*

I often listen to it. I used to love going to night-clubs… dancing. But then I met Darren. I married much too young…

***LOUISE-LISA** holds **JARVIS** and they dance/sway.*

JARVIS moves unsteadily from foot to foot. *LOUISE-LISA* is reliving her youth. After a few minutes *LISA-LOUISE* says.

LISA- LOUISE: Come on!

Alexa, go to sleep.

LISA-LOUISE leads *JARVIS*, now only dressed in suit trousers, to the door (and to the bedroom). Moments later they have left the room by the door (RC) – they do not turn out the light.

AMY stands up and sighs with relief.

AMY(to self but out loud): Thank God for that, I thought they'd never leave!

AMY spends some minutes looking at the photographs she has taken on her digital camera. She smiles. Then she calmly walks towards the door and front door (UL). She sees *LISA-LOUISE's* handbag, which has been carelessly flung down. She picks it up and rifles through the contents which she places on the cabinet: there's make-up, a diary, mobile phone etc – she looks at these. She flicks through the diary and then she uses *LISA-LOUISE'S* date of birth to access her mobile phone. She scrolls through text messages etc. She takes a notepad out of her pocket and she writes something down. She puts the contents back in the handbag and then she carefully places the handbag back where it was in the corner. She leaves the house closing the door and front door gently behind her.

Curtain.

ACT 1

SCENE THREE

THE LITTLEWORTH'S LIVING ROOM IS NOW IN DARKNESS – IT is the early hours of the morning. **RICK** *enters the house through the front door which is UL. He walks into the living room carrying a large black holdall which is quite heavy. He turns on the light. The room has been cleaned up and the drinks and* **JARVIS** *'clothes have gone but suddenly his attention is drawn to* **JARVIS'** *tie which is on the floor by the leather sofa. He stares at it transfixed.*

LISA-LOUISE(*off-stage*): Rick, Rick, is that you, darling? Rick?

RICK *doesn't reply – he is staring at the tie.* **LISA-LOUISE** *pushes open the door which leads from the bedrooms (RC).* **RICK** *suddenly panics and throws the black holdall behind the cabinet (LC) just as* **LISA-LOUISE** *enters; she is wearing a dressing gown which she's tying up over a skimpy satin night dress.*

Goodness Rick, it is 2.30am, where have you been?

RICK:Out...out with a friend – I lost track of time.

LISA-LOUISE: You always say you've not got any friends!

RICK: I've not – there's a guy at D. J's – Andrew – we've started playing cards together.

LISA-LOUISE: What sort of cards?

RICK(*walking further into room*): Blimey, have I just walked into an episode of Midsomer Murders? What role are you playing? Chief Inspector Barnaby?

LISA-LOUISE: Don't be like that, I'm just concerned that's all.

RICK: Aren't I entitled to a night out with a friend?

LISA-LOUISE: Of course you are, Sweetheart! You just never tell me that's all: no phone calls, no texts, nothing.

RICK: I don't like mobile phones – people are on them constantly – they've killed the art of conversation. Stone dead. They're the work of Satan.

LISA-LOUISE: Well Satan would have a job connecting with you – your phone's always switched off.

RICK: I told you, I don't like them – no one ever wants to contact me anyway.

LISA-LOUISE: I do! I worry about you when you're so late home – you're always out these days… particularly on Wednesday and Saturday nights…

LISA-LOUISE'S *eyes follow* ***RICK'S*** *to the tie on the floor.*

Goodness, what's that?

RICK: I'm no expert but it looks to me like a lesser spotted viper – oh no… closer inspection suggests it's a gentleman's tie.

LISA-LOUISE and *RICK* both go to grab the tie at the same time. *LISA-LOUISE* is quicker and she snatches it up from the floor and stuffs it in the pocket of her dressing gown.

LISA-LOUISE: No need for sarcasm.

RICK: Well, it's not one of mine so whose been here… whilst I've been out playing poker with Charles.

LISA-LOUISE: I thought you said his name was Andrew?

RICK: Charles Andrews – with an "S" - everyone at D. J's is known by their surname – it's a legacy from the old days – Mr Butt senior is like that.

(*beat*)

You're not answering the question, who's been here?

LISA-LOUISE: Been here? What do you mean?

RICK: Look Lisa-Louise, I don't want to get all Sherlock Holmes on you but I enter our house at approximately 2.30am and walk into the living room where I see a man's tie lying on the floor and my wife, who can normally sleep through a tsunami, gets up as soon as she hears my key in the lock – you don't normally wake up when I get home late. That indicates to me that someone has been here and probably left before you went into the deep REM stage of sleep which to you is one step down from a full-blown coma.

LISA-LOUISE: I was sound asleep but I woke up – I had a bad dream – even after all this time I still have visions of Darren crashing into that rocky outcrop in Fuerteventura – I think it's called Post-Traumatic Stress Syndrome.

RICK: OK, that may explain why you woke up but it doesn't explain why there's a tie on our living room floor, does it?

LISA-LOUISE: You're just being paranoid, Rick, who would have been here?

RICK: Clive Delavero for a start.

*LISA-LOUISE turns away and walks towards the kitchen area (RC) and (UR) so she has her back to **RICK**.*

LISA-LOUISE: You're just being silly… anyway, Clive wasn't in work today, he went to see England at Twickenham.

RICK: What were they doing there?

LISA-LOUISE: Playing rugby, I believe. Jarvis was in charge.

RICK: That snake – he's about as useful as a fork with no prongs.

LISA-LOUISE(*laughs*): He is too! Do you know what? He's only ever had two girlfriends and he won't take a girlfriend home now because of his Dad's womanising – he's actually quite insecure - all bluff and bluster. Total opposite to Clive.

RICK: You should go on Strictly Come Dancing.

LISA-LOUISE: Why?

RICK: Because you're an expert at the sidestep – especially when it comes to answering questions.

*(With a sudden burst of anger **RICK** marches up to **LISA-LOUISE**, who is now by the kitchenette area (UR) and grabs hold of her by the arm - he roughly turns her around.)*

Now tell me Lisa-Louise – whose is that bloody tie which is now in the pocket of your dressing gown?

LISA-LOUISE: It's… its…its…Darren's.

RICK: Darren's?

LISA-LOUISE: Darren's.

RICK: Darren's?

LISA-LOUISE: Darren's.

RICK: Darren's?

But he's been dead fifteen years! What the Hell did he do? Forget to wear a tie when he got killed on a jet ski in Fuerteventura? Has his ghost come back to collect it?

LISA-LOUISE: Now you're just being stupid!

RICK: Me! I'm being stupid? How the Hell did a tie, belonging to a man whose been deceased for fifteen years, end up on *our* living room carpet?

LISA-LOUISE: I know it sounds crazy but when I got back from work today… well, I was at a loose end – you weren't about – I never see you these days – I was lonely so I decided to tidy the loft.

RICK: The loft?

LISA-LOUISE: Yes, the loft.

RICK: When most people are at a loose end, they download a film from Amazon Prime, Sky or Netflix!

LISA-LOUISE: I wanted to have a clear out. We had one of those charity bags come through the door the other day – Red Cross, Kids with Cancer, Save the Hump-backed whale – that sort of thing.

RICK: So, let's get this straight - Delavero's closes at 4pm on a Saturday, no doubt you went to the Red Lion and had a drink and a meal – then, you get home between seven and eight – for the sake of argument - and think to yourself – (*mimicking LISA-LOUISE*) "I know I'm at a loose end – I'll fill up one of those charity bags that came through the door the other day."

LISA-LOUISE: Yes, yes, that's about the size of it – I didn't realise there was still some of Darren's clothes in the loft.

RICK: Nor did I and I go up there more often than you do. In fact, all we have up there are Christmas decorations and suitcases – so tell me Lisa-Louise, where exactly in the loft was this big bag of Darren's old clothes? Bearing in mind I have a lot of them in my wardrobe.

LISA-LOUISE: Umm...he would like that. He was keen on re-cycling even before it became uber trendy.

RICK: So coming back to this tie, Lisa-Louise, I'm waiting for your explanation of how it ended up on the living room floor.

LISA-LOUISE: Well, it was stuck on the Christmas decorations. I just saw it there looking so forlorn – over a sprig of plastic mistletoe – it was kinda poignant – Darren wasn't all that... but well... we did have our moments together and he perished so tragically at sea. I think it was the tie that led to me having a nightmare about his accident.

RICK: So you went to the loft to clear it out, even though there is actually not much in it. That involved getting the steps, lifting the hatch, pulling the ladder down – something I've seen you do once in fourteen years of marriage - and you came back down with one – *just one* - of Darren's ties?

LISA-LOUISE: Yes... yes... exactly.

RICK: So how did it end up on the living room floor?

LISA-LOUISE: It fell out of the bag.

RICK: One tie? Fell out of a plastic charity bag?

LISA-LOUISE(*laughs*): Oh, don't be so silly! I cleared out some of my clothes too! Out of the wardrobes in our bedroom – trousers, skirts, shoes, blouses, dresses – that sort of thing – things I don't wear anymore! Then I thought I would look up in the loft, you know, just to see if there was anything else. I think it was having that new bed delivered that made me think of it – the clear-out I mean – I thought it was time for a Spring clean – I know it's November but it's never too late... or too early... and then the plastic charity bag came through the door.... Well, it was like, it was like.... Devine intervention.

RICK: The Almighty clearly sets his sights extremely low these days.

Where's the charity bag now?

LISA-LOUISE: In the garage.

RICK: So the charity collectors have a key to our garage, do they?

LISA-LOUISE: Rick, you're being purposefully obtuse. Charities don't work weekends! Everyone knows that, they can only afford to work Monday to Friday. I'll drag it out on Monday and leave it for them at the top of the drive.

RICK: You don't normally go into the garage.

LISA-LOUISE: I didn't want to leave it outside just in case someone stole it. You hear so many terrible stories these days of people stealing things – even from charities.

RICK: Good luck to 'um.

LISA-LOUISE: But think of all those kids with cancer or all those poor people in Syrian refugee camps who wouldn't be saved if the bag was stolen?

RICK: Fuck 'um.

LISA-LOUISE: Heartless.

RICK(*walking away from* **LISA-LOUISE** *(C) and (DC)*): There's too many charities anyway. If you gave to every charity that asked for a donation, you'd be a charity case yourself.

LISA-LOUISE: It's about being selective – supporting your favourite ones – like the Royal Family.

RICK(*yawning*): Charities get too much money.

LISA-LOUISE: No they don't! We should all do our bit – think of others and all that…

RICK: Alright then, you've convinced me, I may have a few bits to add to it – there's some of my old motorcycle clobber in the garage which I want to get rid of –waterproofs - that sort of thing.

RICK *goes to the sofa and sits down – he picks up the TV remote and turns on the television.*

LISA-LOUISE: No, no you can't do that, the bag's full.

RICK: I'll put them in a black plastic sack and leave it with your bag.

LISA-LOUISE: The dustman will take it.

RICK: They don't come until Thursday.

LISA-LOUISE: I know but it says on the charity bag

that they'll only take things that are in one of their own branded and sealed charity bags – no black sacks.

RICK: OK, I'll have to await the arrival of another charity bag. I hope it's RNLI and then I'd be helping to save people like Darren who end up in a watery grave because they've crashed into rocks whilst studying the undercarriages of para-gliders.

LISA-LOUISE: That's below the belt.

RICK: So is your story, Lisa-Louise.

LISA-LOUISE: Well, that's the truth, take it or leave it.

RICK: I'll leave it, thanks.

Pause.

LISA-LOUISE: Are you going to put your motor-bike in the garage tonight?

RICK: No, I don't normally, why do you ask?

LISA-LOUISE: I don't want you running over the bag.

RICK: You'll be pleased to hear that Honda fixed a fully functioning headlight to my motorbike and I can see obstructions very clearly. Not forgetting that Reg "Sparky" Hughes installed multiple high-quality lights in the garage when he re-wired the house.

LISA-LOUISE: Yes, I'm not sure why you needed quite so many lights out there – ours is the only garage in Knobsworth with spotlights in the ceiling.

RICK: I like to see my Commando in all its chrome gleaming glory - I don't like shadows.

LISA-LOUISE: Yes, you're a bit anal like that. I think you love that bike more than me.

RICK: At least my Norton doesn't lie to me, Lisa-Louise – the Commando doesn't tell tall stories

LISA-LOUISE: It's not a tall story!

(*There's sound from the TV*)

RICK: Whatever. (*Pause*) (*Yawning*) Anyway, I didn't go out on my bike tonight – my friend collected me.

LISA-LOUISE: Andrew Charles?

RICK: Charles Andrews.

LISA-LOUISE: Oh sorry, it's so confusing when people have surnames that could be first names and vice versa – I think it should be banned - I knew a Chinese girl at school called Yu Fuk – everyone always got that around the wrong way too.

RICK: I bet they did.

(*pause*).

Did you really put a charity bag in the garage?

LISA-LOUISE: Yes, I told you – I pulled it right up to the garage doors - stupid of me to leave it there, I know...

RICK: Did you? I mean when you were in the garage... look around?

LISA-LOUISE: No. Not really. Why?

RICK: I just wondered if you saw the old wardrobe you and Darren used to have... the one... where I keep my tools and motorbike leathers?

LISA-LOUISE: Can't say I noticed.

RICK: You saw the engine on the bench though, right?

LISA-LOUISE: Yes, yes of course.

RICK: It looked OK?

LISA-LOUISE(*laughing*): Why wouldn't it? It hasn't

worked for four years – it's hardly going to start itself up and drive off into the sunset, is it?

RICK: No, no, sure, stupid of me – I just wondered if…. if I'd left anything on the bench, that's all, I was working on it and Andrew…. I mean Mr Andrews… or Charles as he likes to be called when we're not at work, came around earlier than I expected and caught me off guard.

LISA-LOUISE: It's a good job you can see the road from the garage with the door open.

RICK: Yes, yes, it is. But I had the garage door closed due to the cold and he had to hoot. I rushed out of the garage grabbing my coat.

LISA-LOUISE: Impatient your friend, Charles.

RICK: Andrews, yes, God, he's an impatient bugger.

LISA-LOUISE: Funny he came around to give you a lift back to his house – that was good of him.

RICK: We didn't go to his house – we went up town – that's why I'm so late – we play in a Poker competition in Paddington. Sometimes I ride my bike around to his house and we go from there but tonight he picked me up.

LISA-LOUISE: Paddington? My, you must be a natural.

RICK: How do you mean?

LISA-LOUISE: Well, I've never heard you discuss Poker before and already you're good enough to play in competitions – from what I hear Poker's quite a skilled game.

RICK: Yes, yes, it is – I used to play it on my own

when I looked after Mother – I've started playing it again.

LISA-LOUISE: Anyway, what does it matter if you didn't clear up the garage before you went out? You're the only that uses it.

RICK: It doesn't – of course it doesn't. I just wondered if I'd left anything on the work bench that's all.

LISA-LOUISE: Like what?

RICK: Oh, nothing.

LISA-LOUISE: What, Rick?

RICK: Nothing, nothing at all.

LISA-LOUISE(*frustrated*): Rick, you are…

RICK: What?

LISA-LOUISE: It doesn't matter. I just can't believe we're discussing this at nearly 3 o'clock in the morning. Are you coming to bed now?

RICK: No, I'll just watch Match of the Day on catch up – I was so busy playing Poker with Charles - Charles Andrews that is - and the rest of the Paddington Poker Pirates – as we call ourselves –- I missed all the results!

LISA-LOUISE(*infuriated*): But you hate football! You say footballers are just a bunch of overpaid tossers kicking a bloody bladder about!

RICK: I know, they are, but my mate at D. J's…

LISA-LOUISE: Andrew Charles?

RICK: Charles Andrews - yes, that's him… well he's a big fan…

LISA-LOUISE: Of who?

RICK: Of football.

LISA-LOUISE: Rick, even with my somewhat limited knowledge of the game I know that football fans tend to support a team, a club – football is very tribal.

RICK: He does. Big time. Loves it. Watches all their games on Sky.

LISA-LOUISE: So who does he support?

RICK: Chelsea… or maybe Fulham or perhaps even Crystal Palace – I'm not a 100% sure – one of the London ones anyway. South London, I think.

LISA-LOUISE: So he loves football but you don't discuss what team he supports when you play Poker?

RICK: Poker is an extremely serious game, Lisa-Louise, there's no time for small talk.

LISA-LOUISE: Even so you want to watch Match of the Day on catch-up at nearly 3am in the morning to see if Chelsea, Arsenal, Tottenham or maybe even Crystal Palace, West Ham or Queens Park Rangers have won?

RICK: Queens Park bloody Rangers? God, Lisa-Louise – I'm impressed! You certainly know your London football teams!

LISA-LOUISE(*angry*): I do Rick, because even though I don't like football I hear Jarvis and other guys in the Delavero's office talking about it – ad fucking nauseum – which I'm sure is the same for you at D.J's - yet whilst I have the tiniest slither of unwanted knowl-edge – you have none. None, Rick, none. Last year when we were on holiday in Antalya the Turkish waiter asked you who you thought would win the Premiership – and you replied Boris Johnson!

RICK: That was a joke!

LISA-LOUISE: No it wasn't! You were deadly serious. When he said he hoped it would be Man U you said you didn't think there was anyone with that name in the Conservative party!

RICK: OK, OK, OK - I've decided to branch out, take on new interests, be less self-pitying. You're always saying I should look beyond myself – have outside interests; now I know I'm not going to beat that Walkers crisps chap on football trivia but I'm learning.

LISA-LOUISE: Learning what?

RICK: About football from Charles... Charles Andrews.

LISA-LOUISE: So you'd rather watch sodding Match of the Day on catch-up than come to bed with me at silly o'clock in the morning!

(*pause.*)

That tells me all I need to know about our marriage!

(*crying*) Oh bugger off Rick! You make me sick! Sick do you understand? SICK!

LISA-LOUISE *exits RC – back towards her bedroom. Doors slam.*

RICK(*to self but out loud*): She's not happy!

RICK *operates the TV for a few minutes until there's the sound of football commentary. Then he turns the volume down and listens. When all is quiet, he turns the volume up and stands up. He walks (LC) and retrieves his holdall from behind the cabinet – he walks around by the kitchenette area which has another door onto the garage (UR).*

*The key is not hanging up in its normal place. He looks confused. He places the holdall down and spends some minutes looking around the kitchen for it – he finally sees it on a kitchen shelf below the window, he picks the key up and he looks at it, deep in thought. Finally, he unlocks the door to the garage, turns on the garage light (which shines through the white blind) and disappears with the holdall. The audience hears noises in the garage. A few minutes later the light goes off and he re-appears, minus the holdall. He locks the door and hangs the key up. He walks over to the sofa and turns the TV off with the remote. He exits through the same door as **LISA-LOUISE** (RC) as he does so he turns out the lights and the stage area descends into darkness...*

Curtain

ACT 1
SCENE FOUR

Later... Monday evening...

*With the front curtain closed **AMY** enters stage left and walks in front of the curtain carrying her golf club. Henry Mancini's "Pink Panther theme" plays. She reaches the end, turns and walks back. She looks behind the curtain and out to the audience – she is clearly looking for someone. **AMY** stops and talks into a small digital voice recorder.*

AMY: It is now 8.30pm on Monday evening and I am patrolling Mormanton Road along by the wooded area and the golf course, which has been the scene of most of The Creeper jump outs. The area is quiet.

After a few moments later she exits stage right.

ACT 1
SCENE FIVE

*It is now the following day. We are back in **AMY'S** office; the rear curtain is pulled across so the back of the stage is in darkness. The curtains open to reveal **AMY** lying on the black leather sofa, she is watching Breakfast TV, eating a croissant and drinking coffee. **AMY'S** mobile phone rings. She turns down the TV and puts her plate down on the floor.*

AMY: Yes… *(pause)*…yes…*(pause)*… yes… *(pause)*… yes… *(pause – **AMY** looks at the phone in frustration as if she wants to kill it)*… yes, Rick, look, I have photographs and they're dynamite – with a capital D – you're going to love it! – or not – depending on what you wanted. But I'm telling you, they're the absolute cat's bollocks - and not what you think. No, No, No, No, not what you think at all! I'll tell you about it when we meet. I'm going back into the field later in the week. Whilst I was on undercover ops, I discovered something else and I want to be sure before I file my report.

(Pause)

I'm not at liberty to say. All I'm prepared to say is that I'm working flat out on this case.

(Pause)

I can't speculate on an op until it is over. If I told you now you would plough in with your size tens and then it would be like closing the farmer's gate after the bull had bolted.

(Pause)

I know you're keen to know who, what, where, when but you've commissioned me to carry out a piece of work and I'm saying to you I'm back out in the field to glean further evidence. I need to strike whilst the kettle is hot.

(Pause)

Just stay calm, Rick … all in good time.

(Pause)

No Rick, I'm not incontinent and I do know what I'm doing. Yes, I know how important it is to you - but impatience is a virtue.

(Pause)

You can hire someone else if you like but they won't do better than me. I've worked like a horse on this case and really gone that extra kilometre to get some absolute cat's bollocks gelignite photos – I can promise you – you'll be impressed. Just hold onto your hat for a few more nights.

(Pause)

I'll upgrade you on Thursday when I've completed my op. Field work is dangerous and risky and I need complete constipation.

(Pause)

Sorry... Rick... it is what it is. I can't be any more helpful I'm afraid...

(Pause)

Yes, I know it's frustrating but you fired me to carry out a piece of work. I'm in the middle of operations. When I've finished, I'll give you a call, we can meet up and I'll give you my full, unbiased printed report - complete with evidence. There's no point me telling you now and jumping off the shallow end.

(Pause)

Rick, Rick, patience, please... all in good time... all in good time...

Curtain.

ACT 1
SCENE SIX

Wednesday evening. With the curtains closed a woman walks across the front of the stage – as she passes a man puts his head between the curtains. He is wearing a Mexican Death mask. She screams and runs off stage right, the head disappears.

Curtain opens.

Later Wednesday evening. We're back in the **LITTLE-WORTH'S** *living room. There's the sound of a key in a lock, footstep, voices off stage.*

LISA-LOUISE(*off-stage*): Don't worry Clive, he's not here – he's never in these days – particularly on Wednesday and Saturday nights – that's why I suggested we meet up tonight. Rick says he plays Poker with a guy he's become friends with at D. J's – Charles Andrews or was it Andrew Charles? I can't be sure - but he's never mentioned him before.

CLIVE(*off stage*): Wouldn't want to come face to face with an irate husband! (*laughs*). That's happened to me a few times, I can tell you, and it's never a pleasant conversation.

LISA-LOUISE(*off stage*): I wouldn't worry about Rick – if he ever attacked you it would like being beaten around the head with a raw chicken.

CLIVE(*off stage*) (*laughs*): It was a wonderful night, Louise – you look divine... as always. Green is so your colour.

LISA-LOUISE(*off stage*): Thanks. It certainly was a fantastic night. You're *sooo* generous Clive. You know me – I'm a modern woman and love going Dutch – but it's so, so, so nice to meet an old-fashioned gentleman who doesn't mind paying for everything. And that bracelet you gave me – well...it's the best present ever... it must have cost a small fortune... and on top of buying me those lovely earrings and necklace for my birthday...

CLIVE(*off stage*): My gifts – I love to treat a woman well, (*laughs*). If I get accused of being old-fashioned and sexist because I insist on buying a lady presents and picking up the tab at the end of the night then I'm guilty as charged and more than happy to serve my time.

They both laugh.

CLIVE DELAVERO and **LISA-LOUISE** *enter the front room.* **LISA-LOUISE** *glibly throws her new, YSL handbag in the corner by the door. Clive is wearing an expensive suit –* **LISA-LOUISE** *is wearing a nice, expensive dress, there is a new bracelet on her wrist. Clive's phone beeps.*

LISA-LOUISE: I'll fix you a drink, what do you want?

CLIVE: I'll have a whisky – Famous Grouse if you've got it – if not Bells or Jameson's will have to do. Bring the water through in a jug – I'll add it myself - it has to be just so.

LISA-LOUISE goes behind the kitchenette area and gets glasses and bottles from the cupboards and places them on the breakfast bar. When she has done this, she says...

LISA-LOUISE: Alexa, prepare a Jameson's whisky for Clive.

ALEXA: *Sorry, I do not see anything to connect too.*

LISA-LOUISE: Nor do I, (*under her breath*) no wonder his first two wives left him.

CLIVE: That's a funny think to ask it.

LISA-LOUISE: Rick bought it for me – it seems to have a mind of its own though – I wouldn't have been surprised if it had sprouted two tiny arms and it had poured the whisky.

CLIVE: That's what I like about you Louise – that sardonic humour.

LISA-LOUISE pours the drinks -a Gin and Tonic for herself and whisky for Clive.

LISA-LOUISE: Alexa, play soft, romantic music from the 1880's.

ALEXA: Sorry, I do not understand that command.

CLIVE: I heard that you cheeky mare! I'm not that ancient!

LISA-LOUISE: What era would you prefer then?

CLIVE: I don't know – Seventies, Eighties you choose.

LISA-LOUISE: Alexa, play romantic pop music from the 1980's.

ALEXA plays romantic pop music from the 1980's.

CLIVE sits down on the leather sofa; he is facing the audience.

CLIVE: Tell me, my dear, do you like being called Lisa or Louise?

LISA-LOUISE: Lisa - Louise, that's my name.

CLIVE: How did you end up with a double barrelled first name?

LISA-LOUISE: I got christened in the Queen's Arms.

CLIVE: Crikey, that must have been a shock for her!

LISA-LOUISE(*laughs*): It's a pub, silly!

LISA-LOUISE reappears with two drinks and the jug of water on a tray which she places on the coffee table. She hands the whisky to Clive and a small jug of water.

CLIVE: Oh, thank you, my dear. Go on, you were saying…

Clive pours water into his whisky – measuring it out like a chemist with a test tube. Meanwhile AMY'S head appears at the window. She looks in at the scene before her and then ducks down and reappears with her digital, SLR camera.

LISA-LOUISE: My Dad used to drink there. My parents had agreed I would be called Frank if I were a boy – Dad was a huge Frank Sinatra fan - and Lisa if I was a girl. The Queen's Arms held a competition – *guess the baby's name?* Of course, Dad couldn't enter, so he told his friend to enter "Lisa" and they agreed to split the winnings. Well, when I was born mum changed her mind and said I looked like a "Louise". Apparently, she had a favourite ancient aunt called

Louise who had the same nose and rosy cheeks. Dad tried to talk her out of it but she wouldn't budge. Then, when Dad next went into the pub, the landlord asked him what I had been named and he blurted out "Lisa… Louise" – and it kinda stuck - that's what I mean I was christened in the Queen's Arms.

CLIVE: I see, you were Christened by accident, as it were?

LISA-LOUISE sits on the sofa beside CLIVE.

LISA-LOUISE: Yes, only it didn't work out well for Dad because "Louise" had been selected by another regular so they had to split the winnings in half and then Dad took half of that so he ended up with less money than a beggar stuck in the Siberian tundra.

CLIVE: Fascinating. I know I've always called you Louise but perhaps I should start calling you Li-Lo for short.

LISA-LOUISE: No, that's not a good idea - I like my fully extended name – thank you very much - I've kinda grown up with it, although I prefer Louise to Lisa… Jarvis always calls me Lisa although I keep telling him…

CLIVE's mobile phone bleeps again. This time he looks at it.

CLIVE: Sorry, my dear…. that blasted Creeper's at it again! I've just had a couple of messages from my Catch the Creeper WhatsApp group saying he has just jumped out on yet another poor woman. What are the police doing about it? That's what I want to know! I don't know why we pay our rates, I really don't! That pervert has been on the loose for eight-months and the police have done bugger all about catching him. Scaring women like that! If I ever caught hold of him, I'd castrate the bastard, without anaesthetic, and nail his balls to a lamp-post to ward off other perverts.

LISA-LOUISE: The trouble is the police don't take it seriously. Because he doesn't physically attack anyone, they think it's a huge joke. When he jumped out on me that P.C. Head could hardly stop laughing!

CLIVE: You were one the first victims, weren't you?

LISA-LOUISE: Yes, he jumped out on me twice - I think I was the first to report it to the police. God knows how many other poor women he'd terrified before me though! They were probably too scared to report it knowing the police wouldn't take it seriously. I think it was the fact he was wearing a gimp suit that made P.C Head chuckle.

CLIVE: A what, my dear?

LISA-LOUISE: A gimp suit.

CLIVE: And what's that when it's at home? Not a suit from Marks and Spencer's, I take it.

LISA-LOUISE: No, when it's at home it's a very pervy piece of rubberwear that conceals the whole body and restricts circulation. I believe it is worn by male submissives who like female domination.

CLIVE: Submissivess, ah, we don't want any of them in Knobsworth…

LISA-LOUISE: No, it beats me why anyone would be into masochism.

They both laugh at her joke.

But seriously, The Creeper is certainly a pervert and it's been going on for months now with only one arrest and that was old Mr Jones who was searching under some bushes with a torch for his lost tortoise. It makes women scared to go out after dark. If I were in charge, I would put all men in Knobsworth on a 6pm to 6am curfew until he was caught.

AMY'S head appears at the window again.

CLIVE(*laughs*): Umm... I think we've been down that road before...but I'd certainly vote for a repeat – especially if it meant staying in with you. I wonder what the miscreant gets out of it? Is it power? Is it a turn on? What do you think, my dear?

LISA-LOUISE: I don't honestly know – these things are often about male power and dominance – perhaps he's some weak individual who feels he has been rejected by a number of women and he just wants to get his own back.

CLIVE: Yes, yes, I see, very profound – but you say he dresses in a suit that demeans him and indicates he likes women to be in charge? That sounds very strange.

LISA-LOUISE: Not all the time – sometimes he wears like a Harlequin onesie and a Guy Fawkes mask and sometimes a Mexican Death Mask.

CLIVE: Yes, yes, I've seen that posted on my Catch the Creeper What's App group.

CLIVE puts his drink down on the coffee table and places his arm around LISA-LOUISE. He gives her a kiss on the cheek.

I bet you're lonely with Rick being out so much. Still, you know you can always call me up – I'll come around, or you can stay at my house, anytime you like – there's only me and Jarvis most of the time.

Although, my step-daughter, Stacey, moved back in with us when her marriage broke down, she spends most of her time at her boyfriend's flat.

LISA-LOUISE: Thanks, it's a nice offer but I like to be in my own house... I'm still married you know.

CLIVE: The offers on the table.

LISA-LOUISE: Besides when I stayed at yours, I know Jarvis didn't like it... he used to look at me... you know... in that weird way of his...

CLIVE: He was jealous that's all.

LISA-LOUISE: Maybe... he's better now.

CLIVE: So, come and stay with me...

LISA-LOUISE(*laughs*): You're only after one thing, Clive.

CLIVE: And what's wrong with that?

LISA-LOUISE: Nothing (*wistfully*) I wish Rick had been more interested in sex: unfortunately, he was brought up a devout Catholic by his mother – his father took little interest in him – and, as a result, he thinks sex is a sin. He didn't want sex before we got married because he said he didn't believe in it. After we got married, I thought things would change but hey... ho... he's just doesn't seem that enthusiastic ...

CLIVE: Yes, it does seem as if people who are not interested in sex before marriage are not so keen on it afterwards.

LISA-LOUISE: That's true. I bought sexy lingerie and I tried to introduce one or two sex games into our fore play – stuff I'd done with Darren like spanking games - he was alright at first and then he gave up – he said he was no good at it but I sometimes wonder if it's me.

CLIVE(*laughs*): You my dear? Any man, most men, a lot of men, would find you irresistible. I know I certainly do, and I can think of one or two others.

LISA-LOUISE: Who?

CLIVE: Well, Spud, whenever he's in the office he can't take his eyes off of your…you… I think you know you're a very, very attractive woman.

CLIVE and *LISA-LOUISE* start kissing. *CLIVE* breaks off.

And we both know that Jarvis likes you. He told me he likes the older woman.

LISA-LOUISE takes *CLIVE'S* tie and pulls him closer.

There is the sound of the front door opening. Seconds later the interior door opens and AMY appears in the room on her hands and knees, a digital SLR camera around her neck, she crawls around the back of the cabinet (LC). LISA-LOUISE breaks off from the embrace.

LISA-LOUISE: He's out of luck - I prefer the older, more sophisticated man.

CLIVE: Glad to hear it.

They kiss more passionately and start to remove clothes.

AMY is taking photographs from behind the cabinet – this time no flash.

CLIVE breaks off.

Tell me about your first husband, Darren.

LISA-LOUISE: Not now, Clive.

CLIVE: I'm interested.

LISA-LOUISE: He was a jerk who split his head open whilst riding a jet ski in Fuerteventura – he wasn't wearing a helmet and went straight into some rocks whilst showing off to a female who was para gliding in a thong swimsuit that left little to the imagination – particularly from down below.

CLIVE: So you married young and were a widow young?

LISA-LOUISE: Yes to both.

CLIVE: And then along came Rick.

LISA-LOUISE: Along came Rick. It's funny we met at a car boot sale in Rickmansworth – it was meant to be.

CLIVE: Rickmansworth near Watford – yes, I know it well – I dated a girl there and cuckolded a husband in a nearby village.

(*laughs*)

LISA-LOUISE: You surprise me, Clive!

CLIVE: Well, you know I've spread my wild oats.

LISA-LOUISE: Yes, a bit like a farmer's muck spreader - aren't you worried the Child Support Agency will catch up with you?

CLIVE: Well, yes and no, a man in my position has to be careful but one can never legislate for a defective rubber.

LISA-LOUISE: Delightful.

CLIVE: The thing is I've good quality sperm.

LISA-LOUISE: Says who?

CLIVE: The sperm bank. I donated. Wanted to help couples less fortunate than myself. Every family deserves a Jarvis.

LISA-LOUISE: Umm, I think the jury's out on that one. You don't still do it, do you?

CLIVE: What donate? Oh no, that was years ago! I've changed since those heady days – now I just want to settle down with the right woman.

LISA-LOUISE: But you've certainly a been a player in your time – even since I've been working at Delavero's you've played the field…. And what about this new girl, Sue? She seems to have caught your eye!

CLIVE: That's just a dalliance… a flirtation… I think you'll find she made the first move and old habits die hard, but I'll get there Louise. I'll get there…it takes time to change the habits of lifetime.

LISA-LOUISE: I wish Rick would change - he was boring when I married him and he's boring fourteen years later…

CLIVE: You must've had things in common?

LISA-LOUISE: I guess at the time we did but I can't, for the life of me, remember what they are now.

CLIVE: That's the same with me and Dora – my second wife – I was just not compatible with my first wife, Janice – she ran off to China with a Huawei executive – that's why I got lumbered with her daughter, Stacey. (*sarcastically*) It's always nice to receive the gift of somebody else's children.

LISA-LOUISE: Janice just upped and left, just like that?

CLIVE: Just like that. Last time Stacey saw her Mother she had taken a selfie on a sampan in Shanghai harbour and posted it on snapchat.

LISA-LOUISE: Blimey – that's not great parenting – it's a good job she's got you.

CLIVE: Well, I couldn't abandon her. And Dora was

like a mother to her. Dora and I started off on the same page but ended up in different books at opposite ends of the library.

LISA-LOUISE: That's like me and Rick. He's OK, he's just a bit dull that's all. He always says he's had more boring jobs than a Black & Decker, but I think the problem is with him. He has no zest for life – no oomph – he has less energy than a corroded, flat battery.

CLIVE: And you're a woman who yearns excitement, Louise – I knew that from the first time you walked into my office, I thought to myself – *"Clive, here's a woman who has oomph, here's a woman who wants excitement, here's a woman that has passion and energy."*

LISA-LOUISE: *"And here's a woman that's a damn good shag."*

CLIVE(*laughs*): That too – but let's face it Louise, it's taken quite a few years…

LISA-LOUISE: I like to play hard to get.

CLIVE: That's what I like about you, Louise, you're in control, you know what you want.

They continue to kiss passionately.

AMY *takes some more photographs and then, on all fours, she makes for the interior door and then the front door. Neither **CLIVE** nor **LISA-LOUISE** have been aware of her presence.*

LISA-LOUISE *breaks off from the passionate embrace.*

LISA-LOUISE: I think we would be more comfortable in the bedroom – I've just bought a new bed.

CLIVE: And you want me to christen it? I would be delighted to oblige, my dear.

LISA-LOUISE: Unfortunately you wouldn't be the first.

CLIVE: But I thought you said…

LISA-LOUISE(*cuts in*): Well, to be honest, it's not that new…

CLIVE: Rick wasn't interested?

LISA-LOUISE (**LISA-LOUISE** *realises she has put her foot in it*): he has his moments – they're just few and far between that's all.

CLIVE: Unless you have another lover – I know in the office…

LISA-LOUISE: No, no, (*laughs hollowly*) I'm talking about Rick, of course. What do you take me for, Clive? Ha! Ha! Surely you don't think I have more than one lover?

CLIVE(*said with slight menace*): Just so you know, my dear, I don't share. Bit selfish like that. Always have been. I understand you're a married woman but I don't expect to be cheated on… I buy you expensive gifts, I take you out for meals - that should keep you honest… to me at least.

LISA-LOUISE(*laughs*): Of course, darling Clive, I would never dream of cheating on you but when Rick saw the new bed – well he just had to try it out…

CLIVE(*reassured*): That I can understand. Now lead on McDuff.

Curtain.

ACT 1
SCENE SEVEN

THE ACTION MOVES TO THE FRONT OF THE STAGE.

RICK enters stage left; he walks along the stage looking furtive. He has binoculars around his neck and is carrying a crash helmet – he is wearing a black, leather motorcycle jacket. Finally, he places the crash helmet on the floor, he crouches down and looks up to the middle, right side of the curtain, his binoculars pressed to his eyes. A white light is shining on the curtain – this is the LITTLEWORTH'S bedroom window.

He watches for some minutes, engrossed.

P. C. MAX HEAD stealthy walks up to him.

P. C. MAX HEAD: Hello, Hello, Hello, what have we here then? Neighbourhood Watch?

RICK stands up, shocked.

RICK: I was just…

P. C. MAX HEAD: Just what, Sir?

RICK: Looking at my mine and my wife's bedroom – I'm sure there's someone else there. I think - she's having an affair.

P. C. MAX HEAD: Well, perhaps she should've got net curtains to stop snoopers like you.

RICK: I'm not a snooper. I suspect my wife's having an affair. I hired a Private Eye but she's about as useful as an ashtray on a motorbike. She gets all her words twisted up - she can't be very good at her job.

P. C. MAX HEAD: What's your name, Sir?

RICK: Rick…. Rick Littleworth.

P. C. MAX HEAD: And your address?

RICK: 14, Riverside, Knobsworth – that house over there in fact!

P. C. MAX HEAD(*ignoring the sarcasm, he points off stage right*): And that's your motorbike there, is it Sir? The one pulled up into the bushes? Hidden away, like?

RICK: Yes.

P. C. MAX HEAD: So, let's get this straight. You live over there and yet you get on your bike and ride 300 yards around the corner to Mormanton Road, which comes off Riverside, so you can park in the wooded area, next to the golf course - which the gardens of the Riverside houses back onto – and you do all that so you can watch your wife in your marital bedroom? Sounds like a very, very tall tale to me, Sir, but then I'm just a humble policeman.

RICK(*frustrated*): I've not been home. I've been doing… doing… other things.

(*beat*)

As I approached the house, I saw Clive Delavero's Audi A4 parked further down the street – he has a personalised number plate – Del 1 - so I knew it was him – I then came around to the back of the house.

P. C. MAX HEAD: And you always carry binoculars with you, Sir?

RICK: Only recently – I want to know if my wife is being unfaithful. I know she doesn't love me anymore but I couldn't stand the pain if she were cheating on me.

P. C. MAX HEAD: And where were you coming from at half passed one in the morning? Just finished your shift with Deliveroo have you, Sir?

RICK: No, no, it's not like that – I've been out and about.

P. C. MAX HEAD: Where exactly?

RICK: I can't say.

P. C. MAX HEAD: Perhaps you'll be more talkative at the station?

RICK: Since when has it been an offence to look into the bedroom of your own house with a pair of binoculars?

P. C. MAX HEAD: Do you know what I think, Sir? I think this all adds up to one thing. You are The Creeper and you are guilty of terrorising the good women folk of Knobsworth.

P. C. MAX HEAD *on the police radio.*

Alpha, Tango, Sierra, 142. I need a car – Mormanton Road, by the woods, I've caught The Creeper.

Pause.

Yes, red-handed.

Pause.

What do you mean? Creeping about of course.

RICK: I'm not The Creeper! You can't arrest me!

P. C. MAX HEAD: I can and I will. It's time, I cautioned you, Sir.

Rick Littleworth, I am arresting you on suspicion of doing something wrong. You do not have to say anything but it may harm your defence if you don't mention, when questioned something which you later rely on in court. Anything you do say may be given in evidence. Do you understand?

RICK: You're an idiot.

P.C. MAX HEAD: Thank you, Sir, I love it when customers dish out insults – it gives greater job satisfaction when making an arrest.

P.C MAX HEAD struggles with RICK – trying to get his hands behind his back and cuff him. RICK is mildly resisting arrest.

RICK(*agitated*): Look, I'm sorry, I didn't mean to insult you, I'm frustrated that's all. Honestly, I am *not* The Creeper, I just think my wife's having an affair – look see, the lights are on, its half past one and the lights are on – if I was at home, we'd go to bed at five past ten – we did that for years - as regular as clockwork – we'd watch the news headlines then up we'd go – well, we used – until we drifted apart like two sticks floating down a river…

RICK and P.C MAX HEAD are still struggling with each other – they look like two mating stag beetles.

P. C. MAX HEAD: And why aren't you at home in bed now, Sir?

RICK(*panics*): I want to find out if Lisa-Louise is having an affair. You can't arrest me – it's not an offence to look into your own bedroom window with a pair of binoculars.

P. C. MAX HEAD: However, it is an offence to be The Creeper.

A blue light flashes off stage.

Looks like our taxi's arrived, Sir. Very prompt.

P.C. MAX HEAD *has finally cuffed* **RICK**, *he looks at his watch.*

Under five minutes – put that in your Comment column Daily Mail.

P.C. MAX HEAD *turns* **RICK** *around and pushes him off-stage to the waiting car.*

Mind your head, Sir.

off stage – the blue light is still flashing.

(*off stage*) I've got a good one tonight, Tony – after eight-months we have finally caught the illusive Creeper. I tell you something, Tony, I've earnt a few Brownie points with the Super. It has been a very good night. A very good night indeed.

Sound of a police car driving away – blue light fades.

Curtain

ACT 1
SCENE EIGHT

IT IS THE FOLLOWING AFTERNOON AND WE ARE BACK IN **AMY DICK'S** *office; it is furnished as before; the plastic golf holes are still on the floor as is the golf ball.* **AMY** *sits behind her desk reading a newspaper. Her trusted putter is still leaning against the desk. There is a loud knock on the door (UL).*

AMY: Come in.

P. C MAX HEAD *pushes open the door and walks into the office in a confident and purposeful manner: he strides across the office and sits in the chair opposite* **AMY'S** *desk without being asked.*

AMY: You must be P. C Maximilian Head?

P. C. MAX HEAD: And you must be Amy Dick? Do you mind if I call you Amy?

AMY: Not in the least, everyone else does, P. C Maximilian Head.

P. C. MAX HEAD: No, please, just call me P.C. Head – no need for the Maximilian.

AMY *folds the newspaper up and places it on her desk.*

P. C. MAX HEAD: Well, Amy, further to our earlier telephone conversation I just want to ask you a few questions about Rick Malcolm Littleworth.

AMY: Be my guest. But I must warn you that, further to our earlier telephone conversation, I'm not prepared to divulge confidential, client information.

P. C. MAX HEAD takes a notebook from his top pocket, opens it and looks at his notes.

P. C MAX HEAD: That may be the case but I'm still going to furnish you with the known facts of the case in the hope that you respond in an appropriate, proportionate and reasonable manner.

AMY(*shrugs*): Whatever.

P. C MAX HEAD: I believe Mr Littleworth contacted you recently in regard to suspicions he had that his wife, Lisa-Louise Littleworth, was conducting an affair – probably with Clive Delavero, who owns the local estate agent business where she works or possibly with Jarvis Delavero – his son – or even with a man called Spud who does the books for the Delavero's.

AMY doesn't answer, there is a period of silence.

P. C MAX HEAD: Can you confirm or deny that I have made an accurate precis of your conversation with Mr Littleworth?

AMY: I am not at liberty to breach client confidentiality. All I am prepared to state is that Mr Littleworth is a client of mine and there is currently an active and on-going investigation which Mr Littleworth has instigated. I might add that, in the words of the great Belgium detective, Hercule Poirot – (*mimicking the great Belgian detective) you have made a mistake most terrible.*

P. C. MAX HEAD: You're not being very helpful, Amy.

AMY: It is not my job to help the police.

P. C MAX HEAD: But what about helping your client? We currently hold Mr Littleworth in custody. He has told us a story which you are in a position to collaborate.

AMY: Collaborate or not it wouldn't prove he wasn't The Creeper, would it?

P. C MAX HEAD: No, but it would help his case. At present I have spoken to his wife, Lisa-Louise Littleworth, and she was only too pleased to assist the police in a manner befitting a person who was respectful of their civic duty. She even showed me her bedroom, at no request from me, where a cursory inspection of the chest of drawers, revealed, buried deep amongst the sensual, satin lingerie and thong style panties, handcuffs and bondage regalia. A further search of the house – with Mrs Littleworth attending and not requesting a search warrant – revealed a gimp suit hanging in the wardrobe of their spare bedroom along with an electric blue evening dress tied up in a Tesco carrier bag at the bottom of said wardrobe which was neither to Mrs Littleworth's taste nor was it her size. That suggested to me – with my policeman's helmet on you might say (*he taps his helmet*) – that at some point or other Mr Littleworth had enjoyed the dubious pleasures of an absent-minded mistress.

AMY(*bored*): Is this relevant?

P. C MAX HEAD: I think so, yes, Miss Dick. Another thing I noted was that Mrs Littleworth told me that she never shops at the beforementioned supermarket due to a Clubcard points failure and would not have a Tesco carrier bag in her house.

(*beat*)

On discovery of the gimp suit I felt a further intrusion into Mrs Littleworth's property was unnecessary but should it be required we will return, with a warrant, and search the rest of the bungalow – the garage being of particular police interest.

AMY(*looking bored*): Yes, I see. Very interesting.

P. C MAX HEAD: Whilst Mrs Littleworth expressed surprise at the presence of both the dress and the gimp suit, she did inform me that she and Mr Littleworth had, when first married, indulged in sex games which had involved dressing up, bondage and all manner of kinky pursuits in which she had played the dominant party – nevertheless, she could not recall whether Mr Littleworth had ever worn a gimp suit during these activities. You might say they practiced a kind of Fifty Shades of Grey in reverse - perhaps they called it Fifty Shades of Littleworth.

AMY(*yawns*): Very amusing.

P. C MAX HEAD: She also informed me, that of late – perhaps over the last twelve to fourteen months or so - Mr Littleworth had become distant towards her and is often home late both from work and from evenings out. He works for a company called D. J. Butt – I believe - where he is a bookkeeper. I have spoken to his line manager who has confirmed that Mr Littleworth rarely works late – in fact, he used the following phrase to describe him:

P. C. MAX HEAD reading from his police issue note book.

"Rick is a nine to five merchant. The only time I have ever seen him do overtime was when his watch stopped for want of a new battery."

The evidence against him doesn't look good, does it?

AMY: Charge him then. It's all circumstantial. A good defence lawyer would drive a boat and mooses through that lot.

P. C. MAX HEAD: Don't you mean a "coach and horses"?

AMY: Yes, sorry, I'm always getting my metaphors muddled.

P. C. MAX HEAD: Although that is not a metaphor – it's an idiom.

AMY: You're clever for a copper – you're wasted on the beat.

P. C. MAX HEAD sits upright, he is brimming with pride and self-satisfaction.

P. C. MAX HEAD: Do you know what, Amy? I have a B. A. – First Class Honours degree in English with a minor in Georgian Ceramics from Durham University. Durham is – as I'm sure you know - a world heritage site with impressive architecture and a Norman cathedral dominating the skyline: in addition, nearby Barnard Castle provides the best eye tests in the whole of Great Britain.

AMY: Glad to hear it.

P. C. MAX HEAD: Amy, you will not be surprised to learn that I'm part of Bedfordshire's NOW Police Graduate Leadership Programme.

AMY: I'm not.

P. C. MAX HEAD: But you will be surprised to learn that, due to my minor in Georgian ceramics, I can identify the manufacturers of a pot or a plate at ten feet.

AMY: WOW! That must come in useful!

P. C. HEAD stands up, takes his helmet off and places it on AMY'S desk. He walks around the room whilst delivering his monologue scrunching AMY'S golf holes under foot. Whilst he is doing this AMY is frantically pulling open drawers and looking through papers on her desk.

P. C. MAX HEAD: Oh it does, not so much for police work but for personal satisfaction. Most pottery – plates, cups, dishes - were made in Stoke-on-Trent - The Potteries – Spode; Churchill; Gladstone – where they still have a fine pottery museum; Aynesley; Royal Dalton and of course, most famous of all, Wedgewood. But like so much British industry it has been lost – Stoke – where I spent many happy days undertaking field trips - is now but a shadow of its once magnificent industrial past.

P. C. MAX HEAD turns and looks back at AMY who has momentarily disappeared under her desk.

Imagine it, if you will – back in the Nineteenth Century – looking out on a magical vista of breast shaped kilns, dominating the skyline.

P.C. HEAD makes a breast shape with his hands.

AMY(*from underneath the desk*): Spewing out soot and filling the populous with carcinogenic illnesses…

P.C. MAX HEAD: Amy, you are not a romantic! Sadly, the kilns are no more – trodden into the dust of history by the march of time.

(*pause*)

Who gives a toss for British pottery nowadays?

AMY: No one.

AMY gets back up.

P. C. MAX HEAD: My point exactly! And that is a sad reflection of how Britain now views its great and glorious past. Take the Police Force – formed by the genius of Sir Robert Peel: it was once respected and emulated around the world but the Force is now but a sad shadow of its former, celebrated self.

AMY: We can pontificate about the dire state of the nation all afternoon but what did you want to talk to me about in relation to my client?

P. C. MAX HEAD: Yes, yes, of course (*he sits back down*) of course. I'm forgetting myself. I get frustrated, you see - I don't think Bedfordshire police always appreciates my numerous talents and abilities – I could have made better use of my B. A. Honours degree - First Class - in English with a minor in Georgian Ceramics.

AMY: I'm sure you could have, but what did you want to ask me?

P. C. MAX HEAD: Sorry, yes, yes, yes, of course – it's just that I don't feel you're being very helpful to my enquiries in regards to Mr Littleworth and his links to The Creeper, Amy. Mrs Littleworth has provided me with compelling information which may indicate that Mr Littleworth and The Creeper are, indeed, one in the same person. Added to which I apprehended Mr Littleworth whilst he was crouched in a somewhat compromising position with a pair of binoculars trained towards a bedroom – which may or may not have been the bedroom of his own house as he claimed – it's difficult to see where one is looking with binoculars. This is the sort of perverted, Peeping Tom behaviour which B. P. P.A.T – that is Bedfordshire Police Psychological Assessment Team - say would fit the profile of The Creeper.

AMY: I see.

P. C. MAX HEAD: Now, whilst Mr Littleworth was not wearing a gimp suit, which is sometimes worn by The Creeper or a Harlequin onesie, nor a Mexican Death Mask nor a Guy Fawkes mask which have also been worn by The Creeper – and we did not catch Mr Littleworth red handed, so to speak, in the act of jumping out on a terrified, lone female we did apprehend him acting in a suspicious way and we now have collaborating evidence from Mrs Littleworth which indicates that a) Mr Littleworth has been coming home at odd hours and b) he has grown distant and cold towards her – I might add a very attractive and voluptuous woman who made me feel most at home and even offered me a cup of tea – a simple courtesy that I note has not been repeated at these premises.

AMY: I'm sorry, do you want a cup of tea?

P. C. MAX HEAD: No thanks, I just had one back at the station.

AMY: OK then, I apologise but I'm not in a position to assist you further.

P. C. HEAD gets up again and starts to walk around the room, he carelessly treads on AMY'S golf holes – he has gone off track once more.

P. C. MAX HEAD: Sometimes I wonder why I joined the police service with the late nights, the shift work, the abuse from drunks when it is chucking out time in the pubs. It plays havoc with your social life – most coppers are divorced – it doesn't suit a family life. Yet, with my B. A. (HONS) - First Class - in English with a minor in Georgian ceramics – well, the world was my oyster. I had many, many opportunities awaiting me – I could have been a city trader – The Wolf of Threadneedle Street - earning circa £6.8 million per annum – that's including bonuses of course; a politician of note or I could have been a respected scholar lecturing students on the history of the British pottery industry and writing worthy, academic tomes. Do you know, I even went to Dresden, whilst studying my degree, and did a thesis on the different potting techniques of the Germanic and English nations.

AMY: It's a pity the RAF bombed the bloody place during the Second World War.

P. C. MAX HEAD: Yes, that did make rather a dent in my dissertation.

Still…

I have ended up here, in the shabby rooms of some wanta be private eye investigating a deviant who goes around at night terrifying women in a gimp suit or wears a Harlequin onesie along with a Guy Fawkes or Mexican Death Mask. I ask you! What a life!

AMY: Charming!

P. C. MAX HEAD: Yet, that being said, Amy, I feel in this small, somewhat humble office, needing decoration, with plastic debris strewn on the floor and lacking the comforts which would make a self-respecting cockroach feel at home the muse of inspiration has again struck me.

P. C. MAX HEAD places a hand on his heart. Then he assumes the pose of a surfer on a surf board - one foot behind the other, bent double, arms outstretched.

(*beat*)

Amy, Amy, since I have been in your office, I have become overwhelmed by the wave of inspiration. I feel I am back at Durham University doing my finals and achieving the highest accolades possible – student of the year; Durham University Debating Champion of the year – two years running I might add; ceramics student to the year; English student of the year; best in class...

AMY: Are you sure it was Durham you went to and not Crufts?

P. C. MAX HEAD: Amy, I will ignore that quip. My mind has once again been switched back to "genius" mode and I am riding the rip tide of inspiration.

(*beat*)

Miss Dick, quick, Amy, take this down please.

AMY: Yes Mein Fuhrer.

AMY stands up and gives a Nazi salute, with forefinger under her nose in a Cleesian manner.

P. C. MAX HEAD: The allegation that the British police are Fascist pigs is far, far from the truth, Amy.

Amy, Amy – are you ready with your pen and paper?

AMY(*sultry, mimicking Marilyn Monroe*): Poised and ready for your for dictation, Sir.

P. C. MAX HEAD: Right, I'm back at Durham, final year examinations, operating at full throttle. Quote…

The British police have been crucified on the cross of political correctness.

How do you like that?

AMY: Yes, very good.

P. C. MAX HEAD: Here's another – I'm really riding the rip tide of inspiration now.

The police are frightened to tread on anyone's toes. We now live in a land of forgive and forget justice.

AMY: Excellent.

P. C. MAX HEAD: And another?

AMY: Yes, yes, this is good.

P. C. MAX HEAD: *The strong arm of the law has been chopped off at the shoulder. The police are now just a bunch of Horatio Nelsons fighting crime one handed.*

AMY: You're certainly on form, P.C. Head, but at least Nelson…

P. C MAX HEAD stands up straight and puts his hand up as if stopping traffic.

P. C. MAX HEAD: Yes, yes, don't say it Amy, don't say it. I know what you're going to say.

Ask me why The Creeper AKA Rick Littleworth commits his crimes?

AMY: Why does The Creeper AKA Mr Unknown commit his crimes, P. C. Head?

P. C. MAX HEAD goes back into his surfer pose.

P. C. MAX HEAD: Sexual arousal, fame, notoriety – now it has hit the national tabloid press the attacks have increased – eight-months ago they were very infrequent. That suggest to me a publicity seeker with a big ego. I'm riding the rip tide of inspiration again.

Here's another quote for your pad.

Autobiographies are written by people who have not reached the required level of fame, fortune, infamy or notoriety to have biographies written about them.

AMY: My, my, you really are cooking on gas. You're so right though, The Creeper is a publicity streaker. He probably wants some journalist to write a book or a newspaper piece about him.

P. C MAX HEAD straightens up and walks around the office again. He is full of self-satisfied pride and self-importance.

P. C. MAX HEAD: Indeed. In my experience, which may not be vast, but is deep and intuitive none-the-less, people like to be written about.

AMY: True and with social media that happens all the time now. Goodness, even a meal can't be eaten in a restaurant or a pub without a picture of the dish appearing on a social media site when it's been served up – oh please, how crass and tasteless is that?

P. C. MAX HEAD: Yes, yes, and if you work for the police, ambulance service or you're a mini cab driver you get to see the meal *after* it has been eaten.

(*beat*)

No one wants to post pictures of that on social media!

AMY(*laughs*): You're so right! I know we've gone well and truly off piss but I've really enjoyed your visit P. C. Head. We both sing from same hymn shit.

P. C. MAX HEAD: You see, we're two of a kind – you and me, Amy, we don't see the world through rose coloured spectacles like the rest of the population.

(*beat*)

We are people apart.

P.C. MAX HEAD walks to the front of the stage and surveys the audience, looking out at them with his hand against his forehead like a sailor looking out to sea, shielding his eyes.

I should have gone into politics – I can see it now - large crowds – perhaps upwards of a 100,000 according to police estimates and 250,000 according to the organisers estimates - cheering my name in Trafalgar Square – *Give Head* (*pause*) *a chance to put things right.*

AMY: Well you certainly couldn't make a worse job of it than the current crop of crazy, crazy, clueless, incontinents.

P.C. MAX HEAD turns back into the room.

P.C. MAX HEAD: I could be in Westminster by now – and I've the advantage that I would write all my own speeches – I wouldn't need a speech writer. I would be a highflyer - marked out for the highest office in the land in ten years - may be less with a fair wind and a head start.

AMY: In the land? Yes, P. C. Head, you could do it. You could do it; I can see you've got the talent.

P. C. MAX HEAD walks around the room, he continues to tread on AMY'S golf holes – she looks aghast.

P. C. MAX HEAD: Sadly Ms Dick, you may be right but I fear that what is fucked, cannot be unfucked.

Whilst P. C. MAX HEAD has been riding the rip tide of inspiration AMY has found what she has been frantically looking for.

AMY: Look, I'm sure it's not breaking any confidence to say that another case I have on my books, which I have to be honest, I'd forgotten all about until just now because my brother was doing some research on it for me - was investigating a fraud at a small, engineering company named D. J. Butt. They've lost £16,000 – probably more – they don't want to go to the police as they feel it's almost certainly an inside job – and of course, that is where Mr Littleworth works.

P. C. MAX HEAD: Ms Dick – Amy - that is very pertinent information to our enquiry. (*He sits back down scribbles frantically in his note book*). At last, you are doing your civic duty and helping the police. I'm most impressed.

(*beat*)

I feel we are now making progress in this investigation and I am closer to getting my first cuff and conviction after two years of dedicated post-graduation police work. We now have the possibility that Mr Rick Littleworth AKA The Creeper has also indulged in company fraud. Now, enlighten me to the confidences bestowed on you by Mr Littleworth: I feel together we can ensure that an innocent man goes free or a guilty man is banged to rights.

AMY: Or an innocent man is found guilty.

P. C. MAX HEAD: For all its flaws the British Judicial System no longer condemns innocent people to jail without good cause. Somethings, Ms Dick, have changed for the better.

AMY: OK. I'll not be breaking any confidence if you repeat your hypothesis and I nod or shake my head to confirm or deny – that way I can honestly inform my client that my assistance with the police was minimal and non-verbal.

P. C. MAX HEAD: Alright Amy, that sounds like a plan that would have the full and unqualified backing of the Chief Constable of Bedfordshire Police. My contention is this: Mr Littleworth approached you and asked you to investigate the following matter – that is whether his wife, namely Lisa-Louise Littleworth – was conducting an affair behind his back. He felt that the affair was possibly with one Clive Delavero, owner, manager of Delavero's Estate agents; one Jarvis Delavero, son of the same or one Spud – name unknown – I did not like to ask Mrs Littleworth about her extra martial affairs when I saw her for fear of causing her further embarrassment – I felt the gimp suit in the wardrobe and the bondage paraphernalia was enough humiliation for one day – not to mention the evening dress which was several sizes too big for Mrs Littleworth and suggested, to me, that Mr Littleworth had himself indulged in an extra-marital affair.

So, to resume, Mr Littleworth only knew the fellow

as Spud – an accountant with, from what I can gather, a dubious dress sense. Mr Littleworth wanted evidence of such and paid you a retainer and asked you to discover whether or not Mrs Littleworth was engaged, outside of marriage, with behaviour unbecoming to a married woman.

AMY nods.

P. C. MAX HEAD: Did he want to divorce Mrs Littleworth?

AMY: That I don't know. I don't think so.

P. C. MAX HEAD: Thank you Ms Dick, you have been most helpful. I have enjoyed our little chat and it has given me the chance to unburden myself of some of my true feelings in regard to the British police service and perhaps question whether, with a B. A. (HONS) First Class in English with a minor in Georgian ceramics from Durham University – is it the best career path for me?

AMY goes to say something. P. C. MAX HEAD puts his hand up.

No, no, Amy, I know you can't answer that one but it is perhaps one of life's ironies that you never used to be able to join the police unless you were six foot tall, in old money, and now you can't join it unless you have a degree which is a 2:1 or above. In the past the police service discriminated against dwarfs, midgets, short-arses and females because they didn't meet the height requirement – the vertically challenged in politically correct parlance - now the police service discriminates against the intellectually challenged. Go figure as the Americans say.

P. C MAX HEAD stands up and makes for the door.

AMY: Will you charge my client?

P. C. MAX HEAD: That is not my decision – that will rest with the CPS or Criminal Protection Service as we call them in the Police. However, all the evidence points in one direction – Rick Littleworth is the Knobsworth Creeper. That, Ms Dick, is a certainty. It's been a pleasure meeting you, but I must continue my enquires.

AMY: Likewise, I need to investigate this long-forgotten Butt case.

P.C. MAX HEAD walks towards the door.

Oh, P.C. Head, you have forgotten your hat.

P.C. MAX HEAD walks back to AMY'S desk and collects his helmet from her desk.

P.C. MAX HEAD: In fact it's not a hat it's a helmet, Ms Dick. But a Head without a helmet – my, that will never do.

P.C. MAX HEAD places his helmet on his head, bows ceremoniously and exits the room.

Curtain.

ACT 1
SCENE NINE

Pre -recorded voices off stage to left and right. Some are factual news reports from Radio Presenter (left) some are from social media (right).

Left: This is Radio Presenter - a forty-six-year-old man has been arrested in respect of offences relating to the scaring of women in the Bedfordshire town of Knobsworth – the so called Knobsworth Creeper crimes.

Right:(Twitter) They've caught the Creeper and its Littleworth - retweet.

Right: (Catch the Creeper WhatsApp group) No more patrols – The Creeper's been caught and I've just heard it's Rick Littleworth.

Left: Radio Presenter update: The Creeper jumped out on lone women over an eight-month period but as The Creeper was always dressed in an all-in-one suit – a so called gimp suit - covering his body and face or a Guy Fawkes or other masks - identification has proved impossible. Police discovered the suspect sneaking around bushes in Knobsworth –

close to the scene of many of the so-called "jump-outs" and made the arrest.

Right:(Facebook) Littleworth's going to get it! They found a gimp suit in his spare bedroom - I don't know why his wife has stuck by him – I wouldn't. Forward on.

Right: (Twitter) It's Littleworth! No doubt about it. He's a weirdo! Retweet.

Right: (Facebook) I always thought Littleworth was a creep – his eyes are too close together!

Right: (Facebook) Whenever he came into the Red Lion, he never bought anyone a drink – he always bought a pint and then sat on his own in the corner reading motorcycle magazines. He was a right Billy No Mates.

Left: Radio Presenter: The suspect has been released on police bail pending further enquires.

Right: (Chorus) Littleworth's The Creeper...

The Creeper...

The Creeper...

The Creeper...

Fades.

ACT 1 ENDS

INTERVAL

HAZEL O'CONNOR'S "WILL YOU?" PLAYS AS WE GO INTO the interval

ACT 2
SCENE ONE

WE ARE BACK IN THE *LITTLEWORTH'S* FRONT *room/kitchenette. The curtain opens to reveal the tail end of a wake – most guests have departed. The front room is laid out as before but there are condolence cards on the breakfast bar and the table is lain with sandwiches. Soft music plays though the Alexa.* **LISA-LOUISE**, *dressed in black, is standing by the breakfast bar. Also present are* **P. C MAX HEAD**, *in uniform;* **AMY DICK** *and* **CLIVE DELAVERO** *in mourning wear.* **LISA-LOUISE** *dabs a handkerchief to her eyes.* **AMY** *and* **P.C. MAX HEAD** *are by her side.*

AMY: I'm so very sorry, I didn't know him well but…

LISA-LOUISE: It's all my fault.

AMY: No, you mustn't blame yourself.

LISA-LOUISE: You told him about my affairs… I feel so, so awful… (*LISA-LOUISE starts to cry*)

P.C. MAX HEAD: No, I think it was the trolling on social media – it was all too much.

AMY: P.C. Head is right – it was social media. The

percolators didn't realise how weak and vulnerable he was due to his low self-esteem and, whilst he wasn't on social media himself, they attacked him through you.

LISA-LOUISE(*crying*): I don't believe what's happened, it's my fault, it is all my fault...IT'S ALL MY FAULT!

P.C. MAX HEAD(*placing a tenuous hand on LISA-LOUISE'S arm*): Not it's not! Don't blame yourself, you're not to blame.

(*beat*)

Even though my further enquires proved that the gimp suit didn't belong to him and he was never charged, he was tried and convicted in the court of social media – in the end he just couldn't face it. I guess he felt he was an outcast and, because he had low self-esteem, it made him feel even more worthless.

LISA-LOUISE(*still crying, dabbing a handkerchief to her eyes*): It's still all my fault...

AMY: What P.C Head is saying, and I agree with him, is that the people Knobworth really sent him to Birmingham, that was the real problem.

P.C. MAX HEAD: I think you'll find its "Coventry".

AMY: Thank you, P.C Head, for working so tireless to correct my use of English... I think you'll find Birmingham and Coventry are, in fact, pretty close.

P. C. MAX HEAD: Amy, you seem to forget...I have a ....

CLIVE DELAVERO(*walking up to them*): Not now, please... this is neither the time nor the place. Are you alright, Louise? Come with me, my dear.

(*CLIVE* places a fatherly arm around *LISA-LOUISE'S* shoulder and leads her to the table (DR))

P. C MAX HEAD: You told Rick about her affairs then?

AMY: Yes.

P.C. MAX HEAD: So it may have been a contributing factor.

AMY: It's hard to get into the mind of someone who's depressed – maybe all the elements contributed. From what I've heard, Mrs Littleworth got messages asking her why she was still living with Rick, which was something he questioned himself, so the social media must have been a tractor too.

P.C MAX HEAD: You can say that again. Everyone in Knobsworth knew he was arrested on suspicion of being The Creeper and, because it was revealed on various sites that the gimp suit was found at his house there were a lot of people that thought he was guilty even after he was released.

AMY: He was shocked to fame.

P.C. MAX HEAD: Don't you mean "shot to fame"?

AMY: Do I? Perhaps.

P.C. MAX HEAD: I'm surprised Mrs Littleworth invited you today.

AMY: I wanted to come. After the incident… well Lisa-Louise came to see me – she asked me what I'd told Rick. She wanted to see the photographs I'd shown him. I know there's client confidentially, but I thought there was no harm in her seeing them now he's up at the Whirly Gates. She appreciated how open I was.

P. C. MAX HEAD: So she didn't bare a grudge?

AMY: No, bizarrely she even offered to pay what Rick owed me! Of course, I couldn't take a penny. I told her about my conversation with Rick and how I had advised him to do some work on his low self-esteem. She said she'd been telling him that for years.

P.C. MAX HEAD: I found her most open and accommodating when I interviewed her having first arrested Rick.

AMY: You can't help feeling a bit sorry for her. Do you know what she told me?

P.C. MAX HEAD: No.

AMY: You know he hung himself from a branch of a tree in the wooded area behind their house?

P.C. MAX HEAD: I didn't but I assumed as much.

AMY: Some jobsworth from Knobsworth District Council had the branch chopped down on the grounds of health and safety! You couldn't make it up.

P.C. MAX HEAD laughs and then stops abruptly, he looks around, people are watching him.

P.C. MAX HEAD: Did you get any further with your enquiries into the fraud at Rick's company? D. J. Butt, wasn't it?

AMY: Yes, in actual fact, if you come to my office tomorrow morning, I'll tell you all about it. It's quite interesting and I enjoyed your last visit – I've kept your quotes.

P.C. MAX HEAD: Thanks. I'll pop in first thing. I've more quotes too.

AMY: I'm sure you do, P.C. Head, I'm sure you do.

P.C. MAX HEAD: No, please, call me Max....

AMY and P.C. MAX HEAD continue their conversation

by the breakfast bar, but the focus now moves to the front of the stage (DC) where **CLIVE** *is standing with* **LISA-LOUISE**, *Clive has a plate full of sandwiches and is eating ravenously.*

CLIVE: You need to eat something, my dear, keep your strength up.

LISA-LOUISE: I don't feel like eating anything – I feel so, so awful.

CLIVE: You're bound to - but time is a great healer. You're a strong woman. You know I've said you can have as long off work as you want. Full pay. No need for doctor's notes and all that malarkey. Just come back when you're ready. Delavero's will support you 100%, you know that, don't you, my dear?

LISA-LOUISE(*crying*): Thank you, Clive, thank you, you've been a rock. I don't know what I would do without you.

CLIVE: I'm just doing what anyone would do in my situation. Life has dealt you a rotten hand, but you'll bounce back.

LISA-LOUISE(*dabbing her eyes*): I do hope so. Wasn't it Morecombe and Wise who said that to lose one parent was a misfortune but to lose two seemed like carelessness? I'm like that with husbands.

CLIVE: I think you'll find it was Oscar Wilde – Importance of Being Earnest – one of my favourite plays and, in my humble opinion, the funniest play in the English language. I'll have to take you to see it one day. Oscar was the best. Plays nowadays are filled with political correctness and psychobabble – the play-wrights aren't fit to polish the great man's boots. I've never seen a modern play that was any good – the authors are just a bunch of left-leaning, BBC loving, Guardian reading, coke snorting, inarticulate junkies.

LISA-LOUISE: Oh, Clive, you're so cultured... that's what I like about you... so many hidden layers... you're like... you're like... an onion.

CLIVE: Well, I'm not a one trick pony, if that's what you mean... my father made sure I had a very broad education. He started Delavero's you know, although on my watch it has more than trebled in size and income.

LISA-LOUISE: And I suppose soon Jarvis will inherit?

CLIVE: Yes, I'm beginning to think it's time for me to step-aside and for him take over the reins. He lives too much in my shadow. I need to give him a free run of it.

LISA-LOUISE: Why didn't he come today?

CLIVE: I don't think he can really cope with funerals, bit immature like that. He's more up-set by Rick's passing than I imagined he would be. As you know I did offer to close the office - but Sue and some of the others - well, they'd never met Rick and wanted to work on.

LISA-LOUISE: Sue...

CLIVE: Yes, Rita, Sue and Bob too. Well, Jarvis volunteered to front it, so I thought it was only fair...

LISA-LOUISE: Maybe it's a good job he didn't come...

CLIVE: I think he finds it difficult... you and me...

LISA-LOUISE: Umm, I'm sure he does.

CLIVE: I know what's come out… with that stupid wanta be nosey private detective over there and that up himself constable… but really Louise (*he takes her arm*) I'm too blame as well. I backed you into a corner. I see that now. It was unfair of me. I trifled with you. Maybe I was scared of my own true feelings. Maybe I always have been.

LISA-LOUISE: I'm so, so sorry, Clive!

(**LISA-LOUISE** *starts sobbing again*)

CLIVE: No, it's me that should apologise. I've treated you abominably. As the great Oscar wrote,

Yet each man kills the thing he loves,

The doorbell rings. P.C MAX HEAD goes to answer it.

ANDREW CHARLES(*off-stage*): I wasn't expecting a policeman, has there been a further tragedy at this address?

P.C. MAX HEAD(*off-stage*): No, no, I'm just paying my respects, that's all.

ANDREW CHARLES(*off-stage*): You knew the deceased?

P.C MAX HEAD(*off-stage*): Only from an arresting point of view.

ANDREW CHARLES(*off-stage*): Oh, so you're the….

P.C. MAX HEAD and **ANDREW CHARLES** *enter the room,* **P. C. MAX HEAD** *is in the lead. Everyone turns to see who the new arrival is. He walks in, awkward, hands behind his back,* **LISA-LOUISE** *and* **CLIVE** *go to greet him.*

LISA-LOUISE(**LISA-LOUISE** *holds out her hand* **ANDREW CHARLES** *takes it gently, unsure, then lets it go,*):

Thanks for coming.

ANDREW CHARLES: I'm so terribly sorry... I didn't see it coming...

CLIVE: None of us did.

LISA-LOUISE: How did you.....

ANDREW CHARLES: Know him? Yes of course, I work with him at D. J. Butt... or worked...

LISA-LOUISE: You're not, are you?

ANDREW CHARLES: Why? Did he speak about me?

LISA-LOUISE: If you are who I think you are then not directly, if you're not who I think you are then not at all.

ANDREW CHARLES: I'm Andrew... Andrew Charles... is that who you had in mind?

LISA-LOUISE: Oh God, to be honest, I'm not sure, I thought he said "Charles Andrews."

ANDREW CHARLES: One in the same. Everyone at D. J's is known by their surname.

LISA-LOUISE: But that would make you Mr Charles whereas I'm sure Rick said you were Mr Andrews.

ANDREW CHARLES(*laughs hollowly*): Did he indeed? He is... was such a playful scamp. I think he liked to confuse.

CLIVE: You can say that again! He's put this poor lady through the wringer!

(**CLIVE** *places a comforting arm around* **LISA-LOUISE'S** *shoulder.*)

ANDREW CHARLES: She'll come through it leaner and fitter. Tragedies either make or break you.

CLIVE: A bit more sensitivity wouldn't come a miss, young man.

ANDREW CHARLES(*shrugs*): Just saying.

LISA-LOUISE: Sorry, I'm Lisa-Louise Littleworth.

ANDREW CHARLES: I assumed as much.

CLIVE: And I'm Clive Delavero.

(**CLIVE DELAVERO** and **ANDREW CHARLES** *reluctantly shake hands*)

ANDREW CHARLES: Did he leave a note? Explain his reasoning for doing such a thing?

LISA-LOUISE: Yes.

ANDREW CHARLES: What did it say?

LISA-LOUISE: *I can't go on, it's all too much.*

ANDREW CHARLES: Short, brief and to the point. Well, there's no point in waffle on such occasions, and its ambiguous enough to leave the recipient guessing. I like it.

CLIVE: Well, he's certainly done that! I'm not sure I like you attitude - you come in here…

LISA-LOUISE: Leave it, Clive, leave it. He's Rick's friend, remember.

ANDREW CHARLES: Thank you, Mrs Littleworth. I've come here to pay my respects. That is all. And I'm assuming, from what Rick told me, that his demise means more to me than it does to you.

CLIVE: I didn't know him well of course…

ANDREW CHARLES: But you knew his wife… Biblically I mean.

LISA-LOUISE: Rick told you… you know… what the private eye… discovered… about us?

ANDREW CHARLES: That he did… and there was more… wasn't there… a lot more.

CLIVE: Yes, well (*coughs*), we don't want to delve into all that now. You didn't bother coming to the funeral…

ANDREW CHARLES: Didn't bother? No. Unsure if my presence would be truly valued if I'm honest and there's more ways to pay your respects than funerals. I prefer to stand alone at a graveside. I don't do crowds. I stand in respectful silence. One minute, maybe two if the mood takes me. Respects paid I go on my way.

CLIVE: Well, that's as maybe but the right thing to do is to attend the funeral and support the bereaved.

ANDREW CHARLES: I don't see it like that. Not at all. Grief is personal not group work. Sometimes, I go into a small, family run café I know and have a bacon buttie and cup of coffee: there I sit in respectful silence, the *SUN* newspaper open at Templegate's racing tips reflecting on those who have fallen.

LISA-LOUISE: We all have our own ways of grieving.

ANDREW CHARLES: Yes, and mine are very private.

***AMY* and *P.C MAX HEAD* approach.**

P. C. MAX HEAD: Sorry to interrupt but we'll be off now. Thanks so much for inviting us, at least we've given him a good send off.

LISA-LOUISE: I hope Rick would've liked it. I thought Father Mulholland was especially sensitive given the circumstances surrounding his death and the Roman Catholic church's teachings on such things.

P.C. MAX HEAD: Yes, I think he'd updated his sermon to meet the requirements of the Twenty-First Century – it's good to see the Catholic Church at last moving forward.

ANDREW CHARLES: In one hundred years' time they might finally be up to speed with current thinking.

P. C. MAX HEAD: You may be right. But I like traditions. I like how things were done in the past.

ANDREW CHARLES: I can see that from your uniform.

P.C. MAX HEAD: What's your meaning, Sir?

ANDREW CHARLES: My meaning, Sir, is that the police have old - fashioned practices and out-of-date techniques – if it wasn't for CCTV and DNA you lot wouldn't catch the blinking coronavirus yet alone a criminal. The boys in blue are all at sea...

(*ANDREW CHARLES* makes a breast stroke swimming motion with his arms as he does so he puffs his cheeks out as if holding his breath)

P.C MAX HEAD: I take great exception to that statement, Sir ... I think you'll find...

AMY: Please P.C. Head... Max... let it go... for once. Think of our surroundings.

CLIVE: Yes. Well said, Miss Dick. We're at a wake not in the locker rooms at Twickers.

P.C MAX HEAD: Sorry.

LISA-LOUISE: Anyway, thanks for coming. I do hope you...

AMY takes *LISA-LOUISE'S* hand.

AMY: If there's anything I can do... I'm so sorry. I wish I could have...

LISA-LOUISE: Thanks. We all do. What do they say? It's a permanent solution to a temporary problem?

ANDREW CHARLES: If life's a bad play why not leave before the end?

LISA-LOUISE: Surely, it's better to stay to the final curtain and collect a refund?

ANDREW CHARLES(*shrugs*): Perhaps...

LISA-LOUISE: Look, Amy, I know you were only doing your job... I don't hold it against you. Either of you.

P.C. MAX HEAD: A policeman's job is to go where the evidence leads without fear or favour.

ANDREW CHARLES: Without fear or favour? Except, perhaps, when it's one of your own.

P.C. MAX HEAD: Meaning?

ANDREW CHARLES: Let's just say your investigations are selective.

P.C. MAX HEAD: I take great offence at that, Sir. The British Police Service is the gold standard in honesty and integrity.

ANDREW CHARLES: Gold standard? I didn't think we had any gold after Gordon Brown sold it all off for bottom dollar.

AMY(*holds her hand up*): Stop, P.C. Head, stop, remember where we are.

P.C. MAX HEAD: OK, I'll leave before I have to call on my skills as the two-time champion of the Durham University debating society to show you that you are wrong, Sir. Very wrong. The British Police Service maintains the highest possible standards of honour, integrity and honesty.

ANDREW CHARLES: Honour, integrity and honesty? My, you really have swallowed the police handbook, haven't you? I bet you're one of these graduate recruits, all wet behind the ears and no life experience?

P. C. MAX HEAD(*bellows*): I've got a First-Class Honours degree in English from Durham University with a minor in Georgian ceramics and I'm very proud of the fact, Sir.

ANDREW CHARLES(*rubbing his ear*): Blimey, no need to shout!

AMY: Come on P. C. Head, I think we should leave. NOW.

CLIVE: Yes, I think that's for the best.

P.C. ***MAX*** ***HEAD*** *and* ***AMY*** *leave.* ***ANDREW*** ***CHARLES*** *casually uses the opportunity to make his way to the table of food and helps himself to a heaped plateful of sandwiches. He returns to* ***LISA-LOUISE*** *and* ***CLIVE***.

ANDREW CHARLES: Nice spread.

LISA-LOUISE: Thanks. I did it myself.

ANDREW CHARLES: Must have taken your mind off it.

LISA-LOUISE: Yes, I find making sandwiches very therapeutic. When my first husband died... well... I like to keep busy.

CLIVE: She made sandwiches for the office and cakes too. Very nice. I put on half a stone.

ANDREW CHARLES(*biting into a sandwich*): Every

cloud has a silver. Mind you, it's the best way to be. Busy, I mean.

LISA-LOUISE: I've always found that to be the case. Rick will tell you... well, I never sit still, do I Clive?

CLIVE: No, she's a right Miss Flibbertigibbet.

LISA-LOUISE(*crying*): Oh God, I just wish... I can't believe it... I should have been there for him.

CLIVE *puts his arms around* ***LISA-LOUISE*** *again.*

CLIVE: Don't blame yourself.

LISA-LOUISE: I can't stop thinking of it. Seeing him. It was so, so awful.

ANDREW CHARLES(*still eating a sandwich*): You need counselling. A counsellor would dig deep, get to the bottom of it.

(*beat*)

You say Rick mentioned me, in passing? What did he say, like?

LISA-LOUISE(*drying her eyes*): You played Poker together.

ANDREW CHARLES: Poker?

LISA-LOUISE: Yes Poker.

ANDREW CHARLES: That's a card game, init?

LISA-LOUISE: Yes, he said you played in a tournament in London - Paddington to be exact.

ANDREW CHARLES: In London? Paddington to be exact?

LISA-LOUISE: Yes, he said you were called The Paddington Poker Pirates.

ANDREW CHARLES: Paddington Poker Pirates?

LISA-LOUISE: Look, are you sure there's not another Charles Andrews at D. J. Butt's?

ANDREW CHARLES: No, no, it's me alright. I'm just surprised that's all.

CLIVE: You mean it's all a fabrication?

ANDREW CHARLES: Well, I can't even play Snap yet alone this Poker game.

LISA-LOUISE: And you don't support a London football team? South London he seemed to think.

ANDREW CHARLES: No, I can't stand football, I think footballers are just a bunch of overpaid tossers kicking a bladder around.

LISA-LOUISE(*turning to* **CLIVE** *and dabbing a tissue to her eye*): Oh, Clive, our marriage is… was based on a tissue of lies…. Endless lies, Clive!

CLIVE: Don't worry about it. Most peoples are.

ANDREW CHARLES: Clive's right. Don't be too hard on him. I guess he felt… he had to… say something…

LISA-LOUISE: Well, why that? Why the pack of lies?

ANDREW CHARLES(*shrugs*): Cards? I dunno, I dunno why he said cards? Were you playing charades at the time?

LISA-LOUISE: No! Of course, we weren't! He'd come home late from one of his regular Saturday night jaunts and he woke me up. After we'd had a very long discussion about the merits of leaving out charity sacks and whether charities were a good idea, I asked him where he had been and he said he had been out with you playing Poker in a competition in Paddington.

ANDREW CHARLES: Oh, I see!

LISA-LOUISE: And when I asked him if he wanted to come to bed at 3am he said he wanted to catch Match of the Day on Catch Up to see if the football team you support which he couldn't name because you don't support a team, had won.

ANDREW CHARLES: No wonder why confusion sets in with exchanges like that! So, you never got to the bottom of it?

LISA-LOUISE: No.

ANDREW CHARLES: It sounds like a muddle. Maybe sleep deprivation had robbed you both of the skills of coherent and sensible conversation.

LISA-LOUISE: I was *not* sleep deprived and nor was Rick.

ANDREW CHARLES: Only a suggestion.

LISA-LOUISE: Can you shed any light on it?

ANDREW CHARLES: Light? There's no light, only darkness.

(**ANDREW CHARLES** *bites into another sandwich, after a few seconds he says...*)

Have you? I know it's early... sorted through his things?

LISA-LOUISE: No.

ANDREW CHARLES: And the garage?

CLIVE: As Rick left it... Louise is too distressed. I've volunteered, of course, but she's refused.

ANDREW CHARLES: So, its intact, as it were. Like a shrine to his memory.

LISA-LOUISE: It can't stay like that forever. I want to sell up. Move away. I can't live here now. Looking out onto all those trees. Every tree is a bad memory. Since Rick… well…I can't sleep and when I do, I have nightmares…

ANDREW CHARLES: Bound to. But shrines don't have to be temporary. Some of the best ones are permanent.

CLIVE: We'll have to clear it out sooner rather than later. The police sent back the contents of his pockets: among the coins and paper tissues there was a small key. I think it's a wardrobe key. Most odd.

ANDREW CHARLES: A wardrobe key? Let me see.

*LISA-LOUISE goes to her handbag and removes the small key, she hands it to **ANDREW CHARLES** who inspects it.*

CLIVE: Well, what do you think?

ANDREW CHARLES: There's a wardrobe out there that's missing a key.

CLIVE: But whose?

ANDREW CHARLES: Mine. I lent it to Rick, he was going to return it.

***ANDREW CHARLES** puts the key in his pocket.*

CLIVE: Here, hold on, give it back. That key belongs to Louise.

ANDREW CHARLES: No it don't. It's mine.

LOUISE-LISA: Did you lend Rick a wardrobe?

ANDREW CHARLES: No, just the key. Long story short he lost a key to his wardrobe and I wondered if mine would fit. They were both Jackman's you see.

CLIVE: Jackman's?

ANDREW CHARLES: Yes, they're to wardrobe locks what Yale are to front doors.

LISA-LOUISE: What wardrobe was it?

ANDREW CHRLES: The one in the garage.

LISA-LOUISE: Why does he lock it?

ANDREW CHARLES: Up and over garage doors are very vulnerable. An experienced thief could enter in twenty seconds, less if they've served time and know the ropes.

CLIVE: Well, you're not telling me a wooden wardrobe door would put up much resistance?

ANDREW CHARLES: No, but home security is all about layer upon layer of defence – there's no one size that fits all. A castle didn't just rely on a moat – even the Medievals knew that.

CLIVE: True. Well perhaps we should go in the garage now and see if it fits.

ANDREW CHARLES: It don't. He told me already.

CLIVE: Well, I still think you should give that key back to Louise.

ANDREW CHARLES: If I did that, I wouldn't have any clothes to wear to work. My jeans and shirt are locked in at the moment. Trapped.

LISA-LOUISE: Do you lock your wardrobe too?

ANDREW CHARLES: Yes.

LISA-LOUISE: Why?

ANDREW CHARLES: I live in a shared house. Never know who's in the next room. They might be honest; they might be a tea leaf: the rented private sector is very transient – all sorts of odd bods come and go.

CLIVE: Never thought of buying?

ANDREW CHARLES: It's hard to get on the property ladder. Especially with my record. Credit is hard to come by.

CLIVE: You've served time?

ANDREW CHARLES: Fitted up. Twice. That's why I don't like the police. There're more bent coppers than straight ones.

LISA-LOUISE: I can see that – the police just make the evidence fit the suspect. I know that from what happened to Rick, he should never have been arrested.

ANDREW CHARLES: Exactly. That's a good way of putting it.

ANDREW CHARLES *has finished his sandwiches; he puts the plate back on the table.*

I'd better be getting along.

LISA-LOUISE: Thanks for coming. Rick didn't have many friends.

ANDREW CHARLES: Yes, I know but we kinda of bonded. We hatched from the same egg so to speak.

CLIVE: Avian or reptilian?

ANDREW CHARLES: Come again?

CLIVE: Bird or reptile?

ANDREW CHARLES: Well, we're both chameleons, so I'd say reptile.

LISA-LOUISE: Anyway, I'm pleased he met you and I'm glad you befriended him.

ANDREW CHARLES: The feelings mutual – he always spoke highly of you. Said meeting you was like winning the lottery.

LISA-LOUISE: Oh, that's such a nice thing to say.

ANDREW CHARLES: He was a nice guy. Decent sort. There's not many about.

(beat)

I take it that door (*he points to the door in the kitchen area (UR)*) leads through to the garage?

LISA-LOUISE: Yes.

ANDREW CHARLES: And you never go in there?

LISA-LOUISE: No. It is… was Rick's man cave.

ANDREW CHARLES(*laughs*): Man cave? Oh, I like it! Man cave? Good one.

Well, I'll be off then.

ANDREW CHARLES leaves the house through the door *(UL) as he leaves he is muttering "Man Cave" and shaking his head.*

CLIVE: What a very odd man!

LISA-LOUISE: Yes, very strange. Do you want a drink, Clive? I can pour you a whisky? I've still got some Jameson's left.

CLIVE: I'll just have one for the road, but I won't stay late. I need to see how Jarvis got on…

LISA-LOUISE: Yes, I think that's for the best. People will talk.

CLIVE: and we don't want that, especially with social…

LISA-LOUISE: media – it's a killer.

Curtain.

ACT 2
SCENE TWO

WHEN THE CURTAIN OPENS ITS LATER THE SAME NIGHT. WE
are in **LISA-LOUISE'S** front room, which is empty and in
darkness. She has cleared up from the wake, although there
are dishes and foil platters etc lying around the sink area.
LISA-LOUISE is in bed. Nothing happens for a few
moments. Then we hear a click and the light is switched on
in the garage. Although there is a white blind over the
window in the door, when the light comes on, it shines onto
the stage. We hear someone moving around. The person
walks into something and swears. There's the noise of a
wardrobe door being opened. This is enough to awake **LISA-
LOUISE**. Although she is usually a heavy sleeper, she has
not been able to sleep properly since **RICK'S** death. **LISA-
LOUISE** enters the stage through door (RC). She is tying a
dressing gown over a skimpy, satin nightdress.

LISA-LOUISE: Hello, hello…is there anyone there?

LISA-LOUISE walks into the living room; she sees the
light on in the garage and places her hand on heart.

Oh My God!

LISA-LOUISE goes to the interior garage door, but it is locked, she finds the key and, with shaking, fumbling hands, unlocks it. She walks into the garage, further into the garage and releases an almighty...
SCREAM.
Curtain.

ACT 2
SCENE THREE

When the curtain is pulled back **ANDREW CHARLES** *is sitting on* **LISA - LOUISE'S** *black leather sofa drinking a cup of tea. He is still dressed in his mourning suit from earlier – although it is dirty and he is dishevelled.* **LISA - LOUISE** *has pulled up a dining room chair and is seated next to the sofa. It's later the same night/early hours of the morning.*

ANDREW CHARLES: So you see, we're both transvestites...

LISA-LOUISE: And you were just trying to get your things back?

ANDREW CHARLES: Yes, Rick used to store them for me.

LISA-LOUISE(*dabbing her eyes*): I don't believe it! Why didn't he tell me he had a passion for women's clothing?

ANDREW CHARLES: He didn't want you to think he was any less of a man – he was afraid of losing you.

LISA-LOUISE: But I'd have preferred it to all this

secrecy – these clandestine trips to London, this made-up Poker party...

ANDREW CHARLES: I know, I can see that. I think he had suppressed it for so long whilst he was caring for his mother and then when he first married you, he didn't want to take any risks - then he met me and it all kinda bubbled to the surface...

LISA-LOUISE: But how did the topic come up at work? I suspect it's not the normal office banter?

ANDREW CHARLES: No, that's for sure. I started at Butt's a couple of years ago but only knew Rick to say 'hello' to as I was on the factory floor and he was in the office. Then, one Saturday, a few of us went up town for a meal and for a few pints as someone was leaving. Well, we were walking along a street in Soho and a heavily made-up woman was coming towards us wearing spikey high heels and a short sequinned mini dress; she recognised me and said "hiya" – just as we passed by like. The others didn't take any notice but I saw Rick looking. Rick knew the woman, who'd spoken to me, was really a guy – in fact it was my best mate, Stevie B. We'd all had a few drinks by then and Rick said he wanted a word in my shell-like. Well, when the others had gone home, we went to a pub and he confessed to being that way inclined himself.

LISA-LOUISE: And you started going to London?

ANDREW CHARLES: Yes, on a Wednesday and Saturday – we went to a support group on a Wednesday and we went clubbing on a Saturday. He'd ride around to my lodgings, or I'd collect him in my car and we would go into town. I knew a hotel where we could change. That's all there is to it really.

LISA-LOUISE: Why did he store your things for you?

ANDREW CHARLES: As I said to Clive, if you rent, you can never tell who you'll share a house with. Even if you have locks on the door you don't always lock them if you're in the bathroom or kitchen or something and anyone can walk in. It was just easier to let Rick store my gear in his garage. I've had my ID stolen a couple of times by house mates who've nicked my post as well as some TV stuff I've ordered mail order. There're so many tea leaves out there it's unbelievable. I don't know what the country's coming too.

LISA-LOUISE: But didn't you say you've served time?

ANDREW CHARLES: Sure, I've been done for robbery and this and that – I wasn't brought up well – no proper morals and boundaries that you expect from parents - but I'm on the straight and narrow now. I've done wrong things but I've been fitted up by the Old Bill too. I'm just thankful to Mr Butt for giving me a second chance. Very charitable of him. I started doing qualifications inside: whilst the other cons were high on drugs, I kept my head down and done some NVQs.

LISA-LOUISE(*standing up*): Well, I'm pleased we've finally got to the bottom of it, but I wish you'd just told me rather than breaking into the garage like that. It frightened the life out of me.

ANDREW CHARLES: Look, I'm sorry, I'll come back Saturday and repair the damage. You 'ave my word. It needs replacing really. Rick never liked using it at night as it was so clunky, he said it would wake the dead – that's why he always came though the kitchen and used the interior door. Of course, it suited him to have a stiff, hard to open garage door – it stopped people going in there. I just jemmied it up a bit and crawled under it, like, so as not to wake you.

LISA-LOUISE: He didn't lift it right up much as we mainly kept our vehicles outside – I bet it's ceased up.

ANDREW CHARLES: I'll give it a proper service, like, put some grease on the bearings - make sure it's working proper.

LISA-LOUISE: What if I'd called the police rather than going into the garage and seeing all those wigs and dresses in the open wardrobe and you rooting through that black holdall?

ANDREW CHARLES: You 'ave a point. I could've been done for breaking in and entry but I stole back what was rightfully mine.

LISA-LOUISE: We'll never know that for sure, will we?

ANDREW CHARLES: I suppose not.

LISA-LOUISE: So, thinking about it, on the night Rick was arrested, he actually had all your alternative clothing – as well as his own - in a holdall on the back of his bike?

ANDREW CHARLES: No. He had a hideout area in the woods for his bag and if he thought you were up – or he'd seen a light on in the house - he would he ride up Mormanton Road and hide it until the following day – he was a belt and braces man.

LISA-LOUISE: He certainly had all his bases covered. I never suspected a thing. (*yawns*) Look at the time! Nearly 4am – it's a good job – I've not got work in the morning but you have, haven't you.

ANDREW CHARLES: Unfortunately not. No. I've just been sacked.

LISA-LOUISE: Really? That's terrible.

ANDREW CHARLES: I know. One of the managers at D. J. Butt hired some bloody private eye to look into some cooked books and missing products. Of course, with my record, I was fingered. I decided to take the rap rather than argue the toss. Well, I lasted two years which is the longest I've been in a job since I left school at sixteen.

LISA-LOUISE: But you're innocent?

ANDREW CHARLES: I am indeed. But that counts for nothing. Nothing at all.

LISA-LOUISE: Poor you.

ANDREW CHARLES: I don't give a shit, I don't want to work there now Rick's well…. He's not there, is he?

LISA-LOUISE: Umm, I can understand that.

Now, I really must get some beauty sleep.

ANDREW CHARLES: Sorry, Lisa-Louise – do you mind if I kip down here on your sofa? It's too late to go home and I don't want to wake up the other lodgers, do I? Then, perhaps, I can make a start on that garage door tomorrow? I'll repair it proper like.

LISA-LOUISE: No, by all means, be my guest. I'll get you a blanket and a pillow.

ANDREW CHARLES takes his shoes and jacket off and

stretches out on the leather sofa. **LISA-LOUISE** *exits through the door (DR), she returns with a blanket and a pillow which she gives to* **ANDREW CHARLES**.

Good-night.

ANDREW CHARLES: Yeh, goodnight. Sweet dreams.

LISA-LOUISE *exits through the door (DR) and back to her bedroom, turning out the light as she goes.*

Curtain.

ACT 2

SCENE FOUR

It is the following morning and we are back in the LITTLEWORTH'S *front room. As the curtain is drawn back, we hear whistling coming from the garage, the interior garage door is open wide.* **LISA-LOUISE** *is now dressed and she is lying on the leather sofa reading a magazine and drinking a cup of tea. Alexa plays soft background music. After a few minutes,* **ANDREW CHARLES** *enters the house from the garage and comes into the kitchen area: he is wearing blue workman's overalls.*

LISA-LOUISE: Alexa, volume down.

The volume decreases.

ANDREW CHARLES: There you are, all fixed. I've replaced the lock with a better one and greased the bearings, so the door goes up and over as sweet a nut.

LISA-LOUISE: Thanks Andrew, I appreciate it.

ANDREW CHARLES: I'll give you my mobile number then, if you want any other odd jobs doing, just give me a call. I'm good with my hands, like, and now I've got time on them I don't mind helping out... for a small donation.

LISA-LOUISE: Thanks, there maybe a few odd jobs that need doing.

ANDREW CHARLES: I've just been admiring Rick's bike. Lovely. Norton – finest manufactures of bikes ever. I love British bikes, me. He certainly looked after it. I can see my face in that chrome exhaust.

LISA-LOUISE: Yes, it was his pride and joy – he was always out there polishing it. Never seemed to go anywhere though - apart from a few conventions – he was a member of the Norton Owners Club.

ANDREW CHARLES: Did you ever ride pillion?

LISA-LOUISE: Once or twice but motorbikes aren't really my thing. Too afraid of falling off, I suppose.

ANDREW CHARLES: Well, if you want to sell it... then I'll make you a good cash offer. What about I give you a monkey and take it off your hands today?

LISA-LOUISE: How much is a monkey? I'm not familiar with cockney slang.

ANDREW CHARLES: Five hundred quid.

LISA-LOUISE: I'll think about it – and I certainly bare you in mind for the odd jobs.

ANDREW CHARLES: Thanks but I would like to have something of Rick's and the bike would be nice. It'd be like a connection.

LISA-LOUISE: You're welcome to keep those overalls of his you're wearing.

ANDREW CHARLES: But the bike would be more sentimental. It would remind me of Rick...

LISA-LOUISE: I may keep it. I don't know yet. Do you want a cup of tea or coffee before you go?

ANDREW CHARLES: Yes, please, and a slice of toast wouldn't go a miss. I'm famished.

LISA-LOUISE gets up and walks RC and UR behind the breakfast bar.

LISA-LOUISE: How do you take it?

ANDREW CHARLES: Just butter and preserve, jam rather than marmalade.

LISA-LOUISE: And coffee or tea?

ANDREW CHARLES: Coffee, milk and two, thanks.

LISA-LOUISE is in the kitchen area, she starts to make toast, coffee and tea.

LISA-LOUISE: So what will you do with yourself now you've lost your job?

ANDREW CHARLES: I dunno, go down the Job Centre, see what comes up. See if I can make an honest crust buying and selling – bit of DIY – that sort of thing.

LISA-LOUISE: Didn't you say you had studied a Level One Diploma in Welding and Fabrication? Don't you want to do something with that?

ANDREW CHARLES: Yeh, sure, I'll look for another job like that, but I'll need something to tide me over. Once you've got a record it's hard to get employment. That's why I was so grateful to old Mr Butt - the last thing I was going to do was rip him off.

ANDREW CHARLES has now made himself comfortable on the sofa and is flicking though LISA-LOUISE'S magazine.

LISA- LOUISE: Yes, I can see your problem. I guess it's why so many ex-offenders find it so hard to go straight.

ANDREW CHARLES: Exactly – no one's prepared to give you a break and if anything goes missing the ex-con always gets fingered. Ex-cons are treated like shit in this country. There should be a law against it just like there is against sexism, racialism and disabilities - its ex-offenderism. You're forced to go back into thieving because society treats you like an outsider, a no-hoper, a leper.

LISA-LOUISE: Yes, I can see that.

LISA-LOUISE comes over carrying a tray containing a cup of coffee, a cup of tea, a pot of sugar, spoon and a plate with two slices of toast on it. She places this on the coffee table. She picks up the cup of tea.

ANDREW CHARLES puts the magazine down.

LISA-LOUISE: There you go. I thought it would be better if you added the sugar yourself, then you can do it to taste.

ANDREW CHARLES adds sugar to his coffee and then picks up a slice of toast.

ANDREW CHARLES: You certainly know how to look after a guy. No wonder Rick was so content.

LISA-LOUISE: Was he? Did he say that?

ANDREW CHARLES: Oh yes! He used to say to me that he couldn't believe you'd agreed to marry him. He was that happy he was. Happy as Larry – whoever he was.

LISA-LOUISE: I'm so pleased. I just wish he'd been

more open. Did he say much about what that private eye told him about my affairs?

ANDREW CHARLES: I know he didn't like the photos, that was the worst thing, and the fact it was father and son, like – I think that was hard to swallow.

ANDREW CHARLES takes a bite out of his toast.

LISA-LOUISE dabs a handkerchief to her eye: it is permanently up her sleeve.

LISA-LOUISE: I feel so awful. I didn't mean to, not with Jarvis. OK, I admit I've been having an affair with Clive these past eight months. Hands up to that one. But Rick was out so much, what was I expected to do?

ANDREW CHARLES: Yes, I can see your dilemma - I've only known you for a short while, but I can see, already, you're an understanding, kind-hearted, liberal woman who would have embraced Rick's cross-dressing.

LISA-LOUISE: To be honest, I know it's not the right thing to say, but I'm not sure I would have. It wouldn't have appealed. I don't mind transvestites, crossdressers or transgendered people or whatever you like to call them, at a distance, but I wouldn't want to be married to one.

ANDREW CHARLES has finished a slice of toast. He picks up his coffee.

ANDREW CHARLES: Well, it's not everyone's cup of tea. I've found that out myself – being an ex-con and a participating cross-dresser makes finding the right mate more or less impossible. I've resigned myself to a life of loneliness.

LISA-LOUISE: Oh, that's sad.

ANDREW CHARLES: In life you just have to play the cards you're dealt.

LISA-LOUISE: As long as it's not Poker!

***ANDREW CHARLES** laughs.*

ANDREW CHARLES: Nice one. I like you, Lisa-Louise, you're very quick-witted. You've got more answers than that Alexa over there.

LISA-LOUISE: That dodgy Alexa Rick gave me. He was always giving me presents – although, now I can see why he bought me so many clothes – he had a vested interest.

ANDREW CHARLES: Yeh. He was generous, no doubt about it.

LISA-LOUISE: We have… had… a joint account but he always seemed to have money, cash which ws unaccounted for. Do you know how he came by it?

ANDREW CHARLES(*shrugs*): I dunno. He didn't tell me.

***LISA-LOUISE** sits on the arm of the sofa, drinking a cup of tea.*

LISA-LOUISE: You don't think, he was involved in this D. J. Butt business, do you? You say it wasn't you.

ANDREW CHARLES: I'd be surprised but you can never tell, with people. It could 'ave been him – he had access to the books. From what Mr Butt told me there was a little scam going on. Someone on the shop floor was making too many products for a particular customer. The customer would pay for what they ordered and then pay whoever was taking the kickback privately at a vastly discounted rate – he mentioned 50%. It had to be someone in accounts as they were able to cook the books so the orders all married up with the materials bought and products produced.

LISA-LOUISE(*suspiciously*): So it involved someone in accounts *and* someone on the shop floor?

ANDREW CHARLES: Yeh... but not me though. I know what you're thinking, but I swear it weren't me. Honest to God. I would not rip off Mr Butt like that. I'm as honest as the day's long (*pause*) well, more or less.

LISA-LOUISE: Well... it may have been another reason for... I mean his note didn't exactly elaborate. He may have realised they'd hired a Private Eye to look into the matter.

ANDREW CHARLES(*dismissively*): Perhaps...

LISA-LOUISE: You don't think that Amy Dick was the Private Eye who was investigating the D. J Butt business, do you?

ANDREW CHARLES: It's possible.

LISA-LOUISE: You see, Amy told me Rick had said he was making plans... he didn't want to confront me because he was making plans - do you know what they were?

ANDREW CHARLES: No – though he did mention buying a caravan or something on the Costa Del Sol – I think he'd got the idea from watching *Bargain Loving Brits in the Sun*. I thought it was with you.

LISA-LOUISE: He never mentioned it.

ANDREW CHARLES: Perhaps that was his plan then – to move to Spain on his tod.

LISA-LOUISE: Spain?

ANDREW CHARLES: Yeh, it's just south of France.

LISA-LOUISE: I know where it is! I've spent many a holiday there - but he can't speak the language!

ANDREW CHARLES: That's never stopped Brits relocating, has it?

LISA-LOUISE(*crying*): I know but he seems to have led such a double life – now I feel I just didn't know him at all.

ANDEW CHARLES: Well, you never really know anyone, do you? And Rick was very private, and, to be fair, Lisa-Louise, you were seeing this Clive Delavero too?

LISA-LOUISE: That's the thing, only recently – I've been more or less faithful to Rick for fifteen year (*sobs*) – perhaps less – but I've only been seriously unfaithful in the last eight-months or so. That's got to count for something, hasn't it?

ANDREW CHARLES: I guess. But why Jarvis too? I think that was a real hammer blow for Rick. He couldn't stand the guy. He thought he was a right little so and so.

LISA-LOUISE: It was stupid jealousy. A new woman called Sue, started at Delavero's – she was young and pretty. We all used to go for a drink down the Red Lion after work on a Saturday and one-time Sue was flirting with Clive like mad and he was really taking the bait. I guess I was annoyed and I started showing Jarvis some attention – I knew he'd always liked me.

ANDREW CHARLES: So, how come the private eye caught you together?

LISA-LOUISE: Well, one Saturday I saw on the

Outlook calendar that Clive had gone to see England play rugby at Twickenham and who had been boasting about the fact that she had two tickets for an England rugby match and she had no one to go with? Sue! Of course, she reeled him in hook, line and blasted sinker (*shakes her head in anger, it is still a very painful memory*) I was seething as he was supposed to be seeing me! When I confronted him, he started quoting Oscar bloody Wilde at me,

I can resist everything but temptation – or some such bloody nonsense.

Well, that just pushed me over the edge. That night, after work, a few of us went for a drink and a meal in The Red Lion. I ended up inviting Jarvis back here. Really, I was just getting my own back on Clive. He's such a womaniser, its untrue - I knew he'd never be faithful. But us women like to try to change men.

There's ring on the doorbell.

LISA-LOUISE: Excuse me.

LISA-LOUISE puts her cup down on the coffee table and goes to answer it.

Sound of a door opening.

(Off-Stage)

Clive, Jarvis, I wasn't expecting you two! Come in.

CLIVE and JARVIS enter the living room. Both are casually dressed. LISA-LOUISE is behind them.

I thought you'd both be in work today.

CLIVE: Yes, well, when I got back from the funeral yesterday, this young man had something to say to me which has rather thrown a spanner in the works; I thought he should explain himself to you.

JARVIS is looking very sheepish; he has clearly been crying. CLIVE and JARVIS walk further into the front room and see ANDREW CHARLES sitting on the sofa eating his second slice of toast and drinking his coffee.

Sorry, I didn't realise you had visitors.

LISA-LOUISE: Oh, don't worry. Andrew has just mended my garage door for me, so I gave him some breakfast.

ANDREW CHARLES: Don't mind me; I'll be off in a minute.

CLIVE(*to LISA-LOUISE*): I didn't realise your garage door was broken. You never told me; I could have fixed it.

LISA-LOUISE: It wasn't... well, not until last night when Andrew jemmied it open.

CLIVE: You mean to say he broke in after I left?

LISA-LOUISE: Yes... and now he's repaired the damage – I think they call it Restorative Justice.

CLIVE: I thought that business with the wardrobe key was suspicious. I knew he was up to no good.

ANDREW CHARLES(*circles his face with his finger*): Yeh right! Is it the face that gives it away or do I just smell like an ex-con?

CLIVE: Don't get smart with me, young man.

ANDREW CHARLES: I was just claiming back what was rightfully mine.

CLIVE: Is that true, Louise?

LISA-LOUISE: Yes... no... well, I don't know to be honest. There're some women's clothes in a holdall which Andrew claims are his.

CLIVE: Women's clothes? In a holdall?

LISA-LOUISE: Yes, you heard right. Rick and Andrew, here, were transvestites, crossdressers, trans-gendered persons… or whatever the word is these days … and still are in Andrew's case.

CLIVE(*clasping his hand to his head*): This is parody beyond parody. Jarvis, get me a glass of water, I feel faint. I need to sit down. Quick!

JARVIS goes to the kitchen area and looks in cupboards for a glass.

LISA-LOUISE: You feel faint! Imagine how I felt when I was awoken by a noise, saw the light on in the garage and entered it to see Andrew with Rick's wardrobe doors wide open and instead of it being filled with motorcycle leathers, tools and waterproofs it was full of dresses, skirts, wigs and make up!

CLIVE: I don't believe it! Rick and this chap are…?

LISA-LOUISE: Yes. And Andrew was on the floor rooting though a black holdall – he held an imitation breast in his right hand which he was just about to lob at me as if it were grenade.

CLIVE: Oh, my dear. That must have knocked you for six.

JARVIS has returned with the water. CLIVE has sat down on the sofa, JARVIS hoovers, ANDREW CHARLES is calmly eating his toast and drinking his coffee.

ANDREW CHARLES: I do apologise for the fright I caused you Lisa-Louise, but I felt that breaking in into the garage and just claiming back my breast forms, brassiere, waist clincher, skirts, dresses, blouses, wig and stilettoes was easier than trying to explain to you that Rick was a cross-dresser and he still had some of my stuff locked in your garage.

LISA-LOUISE: Yes, yes, I can see that, I'm glad it has all come out – it would've been a dreadful shock if I had just opened the wardrobe…

*ANDREW CHARLES gets up, he has finished his coffee and toast, he takes his plate and cup to the breakfast bar and puts them down, he then walks back to where **LISA-LOUISE** stands, by the sofa, and fumbles under the overalls for his suit pocket. He takes out the wardrobe key and gives it to **LISA-LOUISE**.*

ANDREW CHARLES: Anyway, here's your key back.

LISA-LOUISE: So it wasn't your key?

ANDREW CHARLES: No, that was just a load of old pony. An opportunity presented itself and so, I thought that if I could get hold of the wardrobe key it would be one less thing to break into: although as Clive said yesterday, a quick jemmy and I'd have opened it in seconds – mind you, it would have ruined the wardrobe door.

CLIVE: Louise, I think you should call the police. Immediately!

LISA-LOUISE: No, I'm grateful to Andrew for coming around.

CLIVE: What with a burglar kit in the early hours of the morning? Terrifying you like that! What sort of a man does a thing like that?

ANDREW CHARLES: A cross-dresser who wants his clothes back.

LISA-LOUISE: Well, at least I now know about Rick. Anyway, what was it you wanted to tell me?

CLIVE: Yes, yes, well, all this transvestitism business has rather taken the wind out of my sails.

CLIVE takes a sip of water.

Yesterday, when I came back from the funeral, I found Jarvis sitting on the stairs in floods of tears - all he kept saying was "sorry Dad" – well, you'd better tell her Jarvis.

*JARVIS has now sat on the sofa next to his father – taking the seat vacated by **ANDREW CHARLES** who is standing next to **LISA-LOUISE**. JARVIS looks down at the carpet, he's rubbing his hands together nervously.*

JARVIS(*whispers*): I'm the Creeper.

ANDREW CHARLES: You what, mate?

JARVIS: The Creeper, The Creeper, I'm the sodding Knobsworth Creeper, alright?

LISA-LOUISE: You Jarvis? I don't think I'm hearing this right. You're the Creeper?

JARVIS: Yes. I know. I feel so, so bad because of what happened to Rick. That's why I couldn't go to the funeral. It's all my fault.

LISA-LOUISE: You terrorised women for eight-months?

JARVIS(*nods his head*): It started out as a bit of a joke and it got out of hand.

ANDREW CHARLES: A joke? You're having a larf, aren't you?

JARVIS: No, one time, in the office, Lisa, you said you'd done some bondage stuff with Rick. I liked you,

you know that, and I was frustrated when you started seeing Dad.

LISA-LOUISE: Hold on, you did it because you *liked* me?

JARVIS: In a way. I hatched a plan to jump out on you. Then, it was my intention to volunteer to escort you home on the nights you left your car at Delavero's because you had no house viewings. I hoped, through that, we'd get close. It was a bit silly really. Anyway, I bought a gimp suit off the internet and one night left early and got changed in the woods by Mormanton Road. Then, as you walked home, I jumped out. Only I couldn't see properly, and it wasn't you! So, a few nights later I did it to you only it didn't go so good, and I ran off too quickly.

CLIVE: Carry on Jarvis, tell her everything.

JARVIS: Well, I did it again, didn't I? You were full of it and told everyone in the office that some psycho had jumped out on you.

LISA-LOUISE: Yes! I even went to the police, Jarvis; it terrified me.

JARVIS: I know and it made a bit of a splash in the Knobsworth Chronicle as the first woman had come forward too. They dubbed me The Knobsworth Creeper – everyone was talking about my "jump outs" as they called them. But I only did it because I liked you Lisa, I really did.

LISA-LOUISE: I remember you volunteering to walk me home, but I said I could look after myself.

JARVIS: Yeh, that's right.

LISA-LOUISE: But why did you keep doing it?

JARVIS: Well, dad wanted to protect you and so he set up this Catch the Creeper WhatsApp Group and they went out on patrols looking for The Creeper – he thought it would impress you. I guess I felt that he'd muscled in on my patch – yet again - and felt jealous - that's what motivated me to carry on doing it.

LISA-LOUISE: But why Jarvis? Why?

JARVIS(*shrugs*): I don't know. I'm always being compared to Dad in an unfavourable light. To make matters worse, when I was a teenager, I was diagnosed, by a psychiatrist, with a very rare, psychological condition called P.A.L.M.S.

ANDREW CHARLES: Come again?

JARVIS: Penis Awareness Limited Momentum Syndrome. When I'm in the toilet – if I'm at a urinal and there's another man next to me, I can't go – it's worse if there are men either side. It all stems from insecurities about the size of my manhood.

ANDREW CHARLES: Blimey, I've heard it all now!

JARVIS: You see my problem? Added to which Dad's always been a prolific womaniser. I guess I've got an inferiority complex.

LISA-LOUISE: So you wanted to frame poor Rick?

JARVIS: No, not at all. I didn't think like that. It was just something that suddenly came to me, I guess because you angered me up. When we were in bed, Dad texted me to see where I was and you started panicking and said, *"Don't tell him you're here, don't tell him you're here,"* I thought you were going to ditch Dad for me, I really did. Then, when I texted back that I was out with a mate you said, *"ask him if he's still with Sue,"* I thought I was being used. Planting the gimp suit seemed like revenge, I guess. I'd already realised the up and over garage door hadn't been closed properly and I'd seen the interior garage door key hanging up in the kitchen - I'm observant like that – I'm like a sponge.

ANDREW CHARLES: And you came back later and broke in?

JARVIS: Yeh, when I left, I drove off, parked around the corner by the woods and then came back with the gimp suit, which I kept in the boot of my car. I crawled under the garage door and came into the kitchen – I'd opened the door earlier when you were in the bathroom.

LISA-LOUISE: So you entered my house, without my knowledge?

JARVIS: I'm sorry. I don't know what came over me. You always said you were a very heavy sleeper but, even so, I was ultra-quiet – a bit like a Ninja. By that time, I had the lay out of the house in my head and I just put the gimp suit in the wardrobe of the second bedroom, without turning on any lights, locked the interior garage door and left through the front door. I didn't realise that Rick would get accused of being The Creeper. Honest I didn't. I feel so bad about it all now.

CLIVE: Didn't you see any of Rick's alternative clothing then, Jarvis?

JARVIS: To be honest, I didn't really look. I'm sure there was stuff on the work bench, but it didn't register. (JARVIS breaks down in tears) I'm so, so sorry for what happened I know it's all my fault.

CLIVE: Yes, well as long as there's no repeats.

ANDREW CHARLES: No repeats! He should be banged up for frightening women like that! Four years minimum, out in two with good...

CLIVE: Utter nonsense! We don't want the respected name of Delavero being dragged through the mire. There's no need to inform the police.

JARVIS(*still sobbing*): I'm so, so sorry, Lisa, it just got out of hand.

LISA-LOUISE: Jarvis, I'm dumbfounded, I don't know what to say. I just can't believe it.

LISA-LOUISE starts to cry again, CLIVE gets up and comforts her.

There's another ring on the doorbell.

LISA-LOUISE(*drying her eyes and secretly pleased of the interruption*): Goodness me, it's like Piccadilly Circus, this morning!

LISA-LOUISE goes to the door to see AMY DICK and P.C. MAX HEAD standing there.

(*Off-stage*) P.C. Head, Amy, what do I owe the pleasure?

P. C. MAX HEAD(*Off-stage*): We have reason to believe that one Andrew Charles Witlow is at this address.

LISA-LOUISE(*Off-stage*): No, no one by that name.

P.C. MAX HEAD(*Off-stage*): Well, we have been to his lodgings and were informed he did not return home from the funeral he attended yesterday. You might know him as Andrew Charles or Charles Andrews.

LISA-LOUISE(*Off-stage*): Yes, yes, he's here, he has so many names it's confusing – apparently, he's

Annabel Candice when dressed as a woman. But do come in?

P. C MAX HEAD*(Off-stage)*: Annabel Candice? When dressed as a woman? Will I have to add trans-vestitism to Mr Witlow's long list of crimes and misde-meanours?

AMY*(Off-stage)*: These days, P.C. Head, wanting to be a woman or impersonating a woman is not classed as a "misdemeanour" but rather as being "trans-gendered".

P. C MAX HEAD*(Off-stage)*: Be that as it may, my guess is that our man Andrew Charles Witlow has also committed crimes under the guise of Annabelle Candice Witlow. In my experience, which, whilst not vast, is deep and intuitive, a thief is a thief whatever the attire.

P.C. MAX HEAD *and* ***AMY*** *enter the living room.*

My, you already have quite a crowd and I see Mr Witlow has prepared himself for my visit by donning a prison uniform in readiness.

ANDREW CHARLES *is now standing by the dining room table.*

ANDREW CHARLES: I've done nothing wrong, which I know doesn't stop the Oink, Oink boys from making arrests when the fancy takes you.

P. C. MAX HEAD: The Oink, Oink Boys indeed. Yes. You'll be meeting quite a few of us over the coming days. This clever lady, Amy Dick, has done some private investigation work in regards to fraud at D. J. Butt's ... the company that was good enough to give you employment.

ANDREW CHARLES: I know and I've been fingered and coughed even though I didn't do it. That's why I'm not in work today – Mr Butt sacked me and gave me a payoff so there was no come back. Happy?

P. C. MAX HEAD: No, unfortunately not. I know they told you they wouldn't press charges. Now, bad news for you, Mr Witlow, is that I was Durham University Debating Society champion two years running.

ANDREW CHARLES: What of it?

P. C. MAX HEAD: It means, Mr Witlow, I've remarkable powers of persuasion and this morning, Amy and I visited Mr Butt, who gave you a second chance, and I was able to furnish him with a long list of your offences.

ANDREW CHARLES: You're not going to fit me up again? Please! Not a third time!

P.C. MAX HEAD: I'm afraid on hearing of your antics - how you used a false name to gain employment... and false qualifications...

ANDREW CHARLES: I didn't use a false name – I just didn't use my full name, that's all – what's wrong with that? And the qualifications are genuine - I studied in jail – and then when I came out, I went to West Herts College in Kings Langley and completed a welding and fabrication course with the aid of a prison grant.

P. C. MAX HEAD: Fabrication? Um, I bet you got top marks in that.

(*beat*)

Well, suffice to say that on hearing mine and Amy's tale, Mr Butt was chafing at the bit to press charges.

ANDREW CHARLES(*despairing*): No! But he gave me his word! If I coughed and went on my way, there'd be no come back!

P. C. MAX HEAD: But did you get that in writing?

ANDREW CHARLES: No. I trusted him.

P. C. MAX HEAD: Trust no one and believe nothing, first rule of life. Second rule of life is get it written down, Mr Witlow, get it written down.

ANDREW CHARLES *stumbles back into the dining room table, he collapses onto a chair.*

ANDREW CHARLES: Oh, please, God, no, not again – I didn't do it! Honest I didn't!

P. C. MAX HEAD: Stand up.

ANDREW CHARLES: But I've just sat down!

P. C. MAX HEAD: Stand up.

P.C. MAX HEAD *walks over to* ***ANDREW CHARLES***. *Reluctantly* ***ANDREW CHARLES*** *gets to his feet.*

P. C. MAX HEAD: Andrew Charles Witlow I am arresting you on charges of false accounting contrary to Fraud Act, 2006. You do not have to say anything. But it may harm your defence if you do not mention when questioned something you later rely on in court. Anything you do say may be given in evidence. Do you understand?

ANDREW CHARLES: You're a truncheon head.

P. C. MAX HEAD: Thank you, Sir, I like it when customers insult me - it makes making arrests more satisfying.

P. C. MAX HEAD snaps the handcuffs onto ANDREW CHARLES' wrists. His hands are in front of him.

ANDREW CHARLES: I don't believe it, I really don't. Why is it always me? What are you gonna do about him?

ANDREW CHARLES nods at JARVIS.

P.C. MAX HEAD: Why? Is he part of your criminal fraternity?

ANDREW CHARLES: No, but he's just confessed to being The Creeper.

P.C. MAX HEAD: Blimey, there's some strange goings on in this house! You've just confessed, in this dwelling, to masquerading as a woman under the name of Annabel Candice Witlow, and now this young chap has confessed to being The Creeper, is that right, Sir?

CLIVE: Look, he's telling lies, you can see the mark of the man, a thief and no-good layabout – I mean he broke into this poor lady's garage this morning.

P.C. MAX HEAD: Did he indeed? Tell me more!

LISA-LOUISE: He broke in to get back some of the female clothing my late husband had stored for him in the garage. So technically it wasn't stealing.

P. C MAX HEAD: But he did break in?

LISA-LOUISE: Yes, using a jemmy, but he has repaired the damage this morning and serviced the up and over door so it is as good as new.

P.C. MAX HEAD: Still, as that door (*P.C. MAX HEAD looks/points at the interior garage door (UR)*) leads to the garage then technically it is an act of burglary. Oh, dear not looking good, Mr Witlow, not looking good at all, something tells me a judge is not going to be very pleased. A lady, in mourning, has her garage broken into in the early hours of the morning by an intruder.

LISA-LOUISE: He wanted to retrieve his breast forms, his wig, which he paid a lot of money for and his bra, skirts and other clothing; I do not view it as a crime.

P.C. MAX HEAD: But I do. And I am the LAW.

LISA-LOUISE: I must admit that when I entered the garage and saw Andrew brandishing a left breast at me in a menacing manner, I didn't think the encounter would end well.

ANDREW CHARLES: I was going to throw it at you as a decoy and then make good my escape by doing a parachute roll under the garage door. The breast form wouldn't have hurt – it's only silicone.

CLIVE(*under his breath*): A bit like Louise's own breasts, then.

P.C. MAX HEAD: Thank you Mrs Littleworth, for being so frank. I'm further charging you, Andrew Charles Witlow, with burglary at 14 Riverside, Knobsworth somewhere between the hours of 12am and 6am, contrary to the Theft Act, 1968.

ANDREW CHARLES: Bollocks to you. What are you gonna do about him then? The Creeper?

P.C. MAX HEAD scribbles in his notepad and talks out loud as he does so.

Bollocks to you. What are going to do about him then? The Creeper?

P. C. MAX HEAD(*P.C.MAX HEAD turns to JARVIS*):

Is this right, Sir? You have confessed, on these premises, to being The Creeper?

JARVIS(*JARVIS nods his head*): I didn't know Rick would hang himself, did I?

P. C. MAX HEAD: Even so, Sir, you are guilty of committing a crime, many crimes in fact. I think we will need to question you down at the station.

CLIVE(*turns away in frustration*): Oh, for God's sake, Jarvis, grow some! I told you to confess to Louise – we'll compensate her in some way and leave it like that.

LISA-LOUISE: Leave it like that! Rick hung himself because of your son *and* he frightened loads of women into the bargain! Women are too afraid to walk up Mormanton Road, by the golf course now, or Dodds Road on the other side of the woods.

CLIVE: Dearie me - he's explained it was high jinks; there was nothing sexual in it.

LISA-LOUISE: That's as maybe be but he still scared a lot of women *and* Rick died because of it.

CLIVE: Rick didn't like what this lady (*he points to AMY DICK*) told him about your affairs.

LISA-LOUISE(*shouting*): What? What? With you and your son?

CLIVE: Yes, with me and Jarvis, in your bedroom.

P.C. MAX HEAD: My, this really is a sordid tale.

AMY: I think it was the social media that really sent him off the ledge though.

JARVIS: There see, it wasn't me.

LISA-LOUISE(*to **JARVIS** – bending forward and yelling*): If you hadn't been jumping out on lone females Rick wouldn't have been arrested, would he?

P.C. MAX HEAD: Mrs Littleworth has a point. Now (*he stands with pen poised*) how do you spell your name, Sir?

JARVIS: Jarvis (*and then spells*) D.E.L.A.V.E.R.O

P.C. MAX HEAD: Jarvis Delavero, I'm arresting you on suspicion of causing women to be frightened by bursting out of trees, bushes and other shrubbery dressed in a gimp suit, a Harlequin onesie and wearing a Guy Fawkes or Mexican death mask, contrary to Section 5 of the Public Order Act, 1986.

You do not have to say anything. But it may harm your defence if you do not mention when questioned something you later rely on in court. Anything you do say may be given in evidence. Do you understand?

JARVIS *nods his head.*

ANDREW CHARLES: My, your superiors will be pleased, two arrests in one day – and at the same address for unconnected crimes – that must be a first for Bedfordshire Police. Have you got enough cars to take us both back to Knobsworth nick?

P. C MAX HEAD: Leave the logistics to me, Sir.

P. C MAX HEAD *talks on his police radio.*

Alpha, Tango, Sierra, 142,

I need a car, 14 Riverside, Knobsworth.

ANDREW CHARLES: You certainly don't have enough handcuffs.

AMY: That's true actually, Jarvis could run off – he got away with his crimes because he was a fast runner – he was on my suspect list and I did some research on him. He was Knobsworth cross-country champion three years on the trot.

P. C MAX HEAD: Leave the handcuff shortage to me, Amy; I seem to recall Mrs Littleworth has a spare pair in her bedroom chest of drawers –they may not be regulation but I may have to resort to using them. Ingenuity is the watchword of the British police officer.

CLIVE: Look, P. C. Head, I don't want to intervene in the smooth running of the judicial system, but what crime has Jarvis actually committed?

P. C MAX HEAD: He's The Creeper, self-confessed, Sir.

CLIVE: No, he hasn't, he hasn't said a word. When you asked him he just nodded his head.

P.C.MAX HEAD: That is non-verbal communication for "yes", Sir.

CLIVE: Ah, but he hasn't verbally admitted to anything after you cautioned him, so the nod of the head could be explained by the fact he has a nervous disposition and suffers from a twitch.

(*ANDREW CHARLES* is moving from foot to foot, agitated.)

ANDREW CHARLES: Nice one Clive, you put that jumped up Jack back in his box.

P.C. MAX HEAD(*Frustrated, P.C. MAX HEAD walks over to ANDREW CHARLES and gets right in his face.*)

Look, Sir, I suggest you button it, or I may have to bring further charges against you.

ANDREW CHARLES: Yeh, right, like the made-up charges you've already brought?

P.C. MAX HEAD(*P.C. MAX HEAD gets so close to*

ANDREW CHARLES *he stumbles back*) You are seriously beginning to annoy me, Witlow.

ANDREW CHARLES: You pushed me! You pushed me! That's police brutality.

(**ANDREW CHARLES** *turns to face the audience*)

You all saw that! That was police brutality! And I was in custody so you have a duty of care – you must treat me in a humane and dignified manner, with due respect for my human rights.

P.C. MAX HEAD: Been reading the prisoners' charter, have we Witlow?

ANDREW CHARLES: I know my rights.

P.C. MAX HEAD: Yes, I bet you do.

(*beat*)

Why are you moving around from foot to foot like a bloody paralytic giraffe on hot coals?

ANDREW CHARLES: I'm desperate for a pee.

P.C. MAX HEAD: Someone, please, take this man to the toilet. It'll be good to get him out of my hair a while.

ANDREW CHARLES: Well, it can't be Jarvis here, he suffers from P.A.L.M.S.

P.C. MAX HEAD: P.A.L.M.S? Good God, what's that? Is it infectious?

CLIVE: P.A.L.M.S stands for Penis Awareness Limited Momentum Syndrome, it's a rare psychological condition. Jarvis is worried about the size of his manhood and doesn't like other men standing next to him at the urinal – it interrupts his flow.

ANDREW CHARLES: If he stood next to me it'd be

double P.A.L.M.S – I'm hung like a frigging donkey – Phew wee!

AMY: I'll take him.

ANDREW CHARLES: I knew a woman would volunteer once they heard about the size of my manhood; you just need to unzip me and plop it out - I'll do the rest.

AMY: Only if you're sure! I don't want any funny stuff though, remember Me Too!

ANDREW CHARLES: I'm in manacles, love. I'm at *your* mercy.

***ANDREW CHARLES** and **AMY** exit via door RC.*

P.C. MAX HEAD: (***P.C. MAX HEAD** looks at his notebook)*

Right, getting back to this Creeper business. I'll put it to you again Jarvis Delavero, that you are The Creeper, Yes or No.

CLIVE: Wait, wait, wait, that will never do, as an officer of the law, you must know you can't lead a suspect into a confession. All confessions must be made voluntarily without undue stress or pressure being applied.

P.C. MAX HEAD: Undue pressure? It's a simple yes or no answer!

CLIVE: You're leading him.

P.C. MAX HEAD: But he's already confessed once!

CLIVE: But he may have changed his mind.

P.C. MAX HEAD: Clive Delavero, are you The Creeper, yes or no?

CLIVE: No, of course not.

P.C. MAX HEAD: Mrs Lisa-Louise Littleworth, are you The Creeper? Yes or No?

LISA-LOUISE: No.

P.C. MAX HEAD: Jarvis Delavero, are you The Creeper? Yes or No?

JARVIS is sitting on the sofa his head in hands, you can't see his face.

JARVIS: Yeh, sure, you know I am. You lot are doing my head in.

P.C. MAX HEAD(*writing in his notebook and reading out loud as he does so.*)

Yeh, sure, you know I am. You lot are doing my head in.

Anything else you wish to say, Sir?

JARVIS: No, just get on with it, do what ya have to do,

P. C. MAX HEAD(*writing in notebook and speaking out loud.*)

No, just get on with it, do what ya have to do.

I'm guessing we're spelling "you" "Y. A" rather than the conventional way.

CLIVE: You fool Jarvis!

CLIVE gets up from the sofa and LISA-LOUISE sits down. CLIVE is too disgusted by JARVIS to sit next to him.

A toilet flushes, ANDREW CHARLES and AMY return to the living room.

ANDREW CHARLES(*to P. C MAX HEAD*): Haven't you finished yet?

P. C. MAX HEAD(*points at CLIVE*): This gentleman, here, is rather holding up proceedings.

CLIVE: I'm just over seeing the smooth running of the criminal justice system. And whilst we're on that point have you thought of all the ramifications of arresting Jarvis?

P. C. MAX HEAD: What ramifications, Sir?

CLIVE: Well, think of Rick, you had to release him, didn't you, not enough evidence. Then look what happened.

P. C. MAX HEAD: This gentleman has confessed, Sir.

CLIVE: But what about witnesses? You need a complainant? Do you have any of those?

P.C. MAX HEAD: Many women have stepped forward to say that whilst they have been perambulating along the pavements of Mormanton Road, Dodds Road and Riverside their journeys have been interrupted by the terrifying actions of The Creeper. Including, if I might be so bold, this lady here, Sir.

CLIVE is standing behind LISA-LOUISE, she is now seated on the sofa next to JARVIS.

CLIVE: I'm not sure Louise would testify against my son.

(*CLIVE speaks under his breath as he squeezes LISA-LOUISE'S shoulder*)

Not if you want to keep your job, you won't.

P.C. MAX HEAD: Is that right, Mrs Littleworth? You have changed your mind about testifying?

LISA-LOUISE: Yes, that's right, I won't be taking it any further. I want this whole sorry saga to end.

P.C. MAX HEAD: I have other witnesses.

CLIVE: But think of the paperwork? Two arrests in one day, dearie me, you'll not going to get home untill after midnight.

P.C. MAX HEAD: Nice try Sir, but policing is a vocation not a nine to five job with an hour for lunch.

CLIVE: But just think what happened to Rick, all that trolling on social media. Jarvis is very, very vulnerable – he has mental health issues and you've already heard about his P.A.L.M.S diagnosis - I'm sure you wouldn't want to be responsible for... how shall we put it?... another (*beat*) mishap.

AMY: I think Clive has point about the social media: Jarvis is only twenty-six, and he's clearly a sandwich short of a picnic. Do you really want to put him through all that? I went out on patrols and tried to catch The Creeper so it's great that he's finally owned up but should it go further? He's no record and I'm sure he's burnt his lesson.

JARVIS: Thanks very much... I think.

P.C. MAX HEAD: OK, OK, you win, I'll let him off with a caution. I don't want another Rick on my conscious. Head up, son.

JARVIS looks up.

Look, Sonny, any more creeping and I'll come down on you like a ton of bricks, understood?

JARVIS nods his head.

ANDREW CHARLES: Are we talking British or American tonnes?

P.C. MAX HEAD: Shut it, Witlow!

CLIVE: Thank you, Officer, thank you, that's the right way to handle this. There'll be no more creeping, I can assure you of that. I've told Jarvis that he can take over Delavero's, starting in the New Year, it'll give him something to focus on.

(*beat*)

Well, I'm glad that's all sorted.

LISA-LOUISE: Thanks Clive, I won't forget this - putting Jarvis before me! The relationship's OFF. And that's spelt with a capital "F".

CLIVE: Louise – don't be like that! I'm just trying to protect Jarvis.

LISA-LOUISE(*crying*): You've really shown your true colours today; I don't know what I ever saw in you! You're just a self-centred, womanising bastard!

LISA-LOUISE *picks up a cushion and throws it at* **CLIVE**.

Oh, go back to Sue! You pig!

P. C. MAX HEAD: Hey! Hey! Hold on! We don't want a domestic!

CLIVE(*picks up the cushion*): I couldn't let Jarvis down.

LISA-LOUISE: But you're more than happy to let me down!

ANDREW CHARLES: And what about me? I'm still under arrest for a crime I didn't commit. Let me off with a cushion too! I mean a caution.

P. C. MAX HEAD: No, you're a villain with a long record.

ANDREW CHARLES: So, fraud trumps jumping out on lone women, does it? You wait till I tell your superiors down at the station what I've seen today.

ALEXA: *Release him! Release him!*

Release him! Release him!

The spotlight falls on **ANDREW CHARLES** *who gets down on his hands and knees and clasps his hands together* *as if in prayer. He shuffles to the edge of the stage, faces the audience, and lifts his shackled hands in the air.*

ANDREW CHARLES: Oh, thank you God, thank you. I'm sorry for any sins and crimes I've committed. I promise to go straight.

ALEXA: *Release him! Release him!*

ANDREW CHARLES: Thank you, God, thank you. I always knew God was a woman. All men should bow down to women's superiority, dominance and general all-round brilliance.

AMY: Well said, as a practising feminist I divorce those comments.

ANDREW CHARLES *now shuffles to* **P.C. MAX HEAD** *and offers up his wrists up to be released from the cuffs.*

P. C. MAX HEAD: Not so fast, Witlow. I think God is merely ratifying my decision to take no further action against Jarvis: I certainly don't think God would want you roaming free.

ALEXA: *Release him! Release him!*

P. C. MAX HEAD: But on second thoughts...

LISA-LOUISE: God? God? That's not God talking, that's Alexa, you pair of numpties!

ANDREW CHARLES: It's Rick then! He's come back to save me from a great injustice.

ALEXA *starts playing the opening bars of the Simple Minds song "Don't You (Forget About Me)" a hit from 1985.*

Hey, hey, hey, hey

Ooh who

Then stops.

ALEXA: *The rain in Spain falls mainly on the plane.*

ALEXA goes back to playing soft music.

AMY: My that is strange! I've not heard of an Alexa go so off piss before.

LISA-LOUISE: Must be dodgy wireless wiring.

AMY: But it can't be a coincidence that two men are potentially under arrest in your living room and Alexa starts sprouting orders. You don't think it's Rick, do you?

LISA-LOUISE: No. It can't be, it just can't…

LISA-LOUISE and AMY go to the breakfast bar where Alexa stands, LISA-LOUISE stands on the kitchen side of the breakfast bar. ALEXA has gone back to playing soft music but then the volume increases and the opening bars of the Simple Minds song "Don't You (Forget About Me)" play again.

Hey, hey, hey, hey

Ooh who

LISA-LOUISE: Alexa, behave!

ALEXA: *Umm, I do not know that one.*

P. C. MAX HEAD: There's some seriously strange goings on in this house! Transvestitism in the garage; theft from the wardrobe; a gimp suit in the spare bedroom; inter-generational sex in the main bedroom and a pervert and a poltergeist in the living room! I'm scared to go into the bathroom for fear of what horrors might lie in wait for me there!

ANDREW CHARLES: I would be too. I pissed on the toilet seat – Amy wouldn't lift it up for me and it's hard to direct flow wearing cuffs.

ALEXA is still playing Don't You (Forget About Me) – the volume is increasing.

Won't you come see about me?

I'll be alone, dancing you know it baby
Tell me your troubles and doubts
Giving me everything inside and out and
Love's strange so real in the dark
Think of the tender things that we were working on
Slow change may pull us apart
When the light gets into your heart, baby
Don't you, forget about me
Don't, don't, don't, don't
Don't you, forget about me

LISA-LOUISE: Alexa – stop.

ALEXA stops. When it speaks again its voice has changed from a female voice to Rick's voice.

ALEXA: *Don't sell my clothes at car boot sales. Give them to a charity of your choosing.*

LISA-LOUISE(*panicking*): Oh My God! It *is* Rick! It's Rick! Oh My God!

Alexa, stop, please, stop!

AMY: It's like a talking will! Did Rick pre-programme it, do you think?

LISA-LOUISE: No, of course, he didn't.

P.C. MAX HEAD, ANDREW CHARLES, CLIVE and **JARVIS** all gather around the breakfast bar - they gaze at Alexa in awe.

JARVIS(*crying*): He's come back to haunt me!

LISA-LOUISE: No, I think he's talking to me.

ALEXA: *Don't sell my Norton Commando, 850cc Roadster.*

ANDREW CHARLES: Damn, I wanted that bike – I would've got a good price for it too.

LISA-LOUISE: Alexa, stop, please! Please, Alexa. STOP!

ALEXA: *Give the clothes in the wardrobe in the garage to Andrew Charles or Charles Andrews or whatever his name is.*

Continuing to play *Simple Minds – Don't You (Forget About Me).*

Don't you, forget about me

Don't, don't, don't, don't

Don't you, forget about me

(Alexa stops. All the characters stand in front of the breakfast bar in a line in the following order: LISA-LOUISE; AMY; ANDREW CHARLES; P.C. MAX HEAD; CLIVE and JARVIS.)

Oh, Lisa-Louise, Lisa-Louise.

(the spot light shines on LISA-LOUISE)

Don't you - forget about me.

LISA-LOUISE: I won't forget you, Rick. (*LISA-LOUISE bows her head and the spot light moves to AMY so LISA-LOUISE is in darkness.*)

Don't you - forget about me.

AMY: *I won't regret you.* (*AMY bows her head and the spot light moves to ANDREW CHARLES so AMY is in darkness.*)

ANDREW CHARLES: Me neither, mate. (*ANDREW CHARLES bows his head and the spot light moves to P.C. MAX HEAD so ANDREW CHARLES is in darkness.*)

Don't you - forget about me.

P. C. MAX HEAD: Never.

Clive, Jarvis, don't you - forget about me.

CLIVE: Impossible not to. (*CLIVE bows his head and the spot light moves to JARVIS so CLIVE is in darkness.*)

JARVIS: I can't forget you. (*JARVIS bows his head – now all the actors are in line further DR, DC, DL*).

(*P.C. HEAD still has hold of a handcuffed ANDREW CHARLES WITLOW. The cast moves forward in a line.*)

LISA-LOUISE: It's time to say goodbye.

ALEXA starts to play Il Divo – Time to say Goodbye (Con Te Partiro).

Curtain.

The End.

AFTERWORD

For further information please visit my website
https://www.colinmayo.com

If you are interested in performing this play please
contact stage plays, details below

PERFORMANCE RIGHTS

The Rights are $100.00/£60.00 + VAT per
performance

Contact: admin@stageplays.com

Printed in Great Britain
by Amazon